THOMAS HARDY
10 LOVERS
50 POEMS

First Published in Great Britain by
Athelhampton Press
Athelhampton
Dorchester
Dorset
DT2 7LG
United Kingdom

1st edition

Copyright © 2025 Giles Keating

A catalogue entry of this book is available from the British Library

ISBN 978-0-9555815-7-1

All rights reserved. No part of this book may be reproduced or transmitted in any form or by any means, electronic or mechanical including photography, recording or any information storage and retrieval system, without permission in writing from the publisher.

Forward by Mark Damon Chutter

Illustrations by Noah Warnes

Designed by Owen Davies

Photography by Howard Payton

Front cover features
Susie King as Gertrude Bugler

Rear cover features
Kate Braidwood as Tryphena Sparks
and
Jonathan White as young Thomas Hardy

Available in the usual stockists
or order online via Amazon or
www.athelhampton.com (uk only)

THOMAS HARDY
10 LOVERS
50 POEMS

GILES KEATING

FORWARD BY
MARK DAMON CHUTTER

ILLUSTRATIONS BY
NOAH WARNES

10 LOVERS 50 POEMS

TABLE OF CONTENTS

Forward		ix
Introduction		xiii
Chapter 1	**Early Loves**	**1**
2.	*A Church Romance*	*7*
3.	*Lizbie Brown*	*9*
4.	*Retty's Phases*	*15*
Chapter 2	**London Frustrations**	**19**
5.	*The Ruined Maid*	*29*
6.	*From Her in the Country*	*33*
7.	*She, To Him I*	*35*
	The Musing Maiden	*37*
8.	*Hap*	*41*
9.	*Her Definition*	*45*
10.	*She, To Him IV*	*47*
Chapter 3	**London Climax**	**49**
11.	*To an Impersonation of Rosalind*	*55*
12.	*To an Actress*	*57*
13.	*1967*	*59*
Chapter 4	**Phena**	**61**
14.	*In a Eweleaze near Weatherbury*	*69*
	At a Rushy-Pond	*73*
15.	*A Spot*	*77*
	The Place on the Map	*81*
	Her Initials	*85*
16.	*Thoughts of Phena At News of her Death*	*87*
17.	*To a Motherless Child*	*91*
Chapter 5	**Emma - Early Happiness**	**95**
18.	*When I Set Out for Lyonnesse*	*101*
19.	*Great Things*	*103*
20.	*Beeny Cliff*	*107*
	The Phantom Horsewoman	*111*
	We Sat at the Window	*115*
21.	*On Sturminster Foot-Bridge*	*117*
22.	*A Two-Years' Idyll*	*119*
23.	*Overlooking the River Stour*	*123*
24.	*The Musical Box*	*127*

10 LOVERS 50 POEMS

Chapter 6 Florence Henniker 131

25. *A Thunderstorm in Town* *137*
26. *At an Inn* *139*
27. *A Broken Appointment* *143*
28. *Wessex Heights* *145*
29. *Without, Not Within Her* *151*

Chapter 7 Emma - The Sadness Comes 153

He Abjures Love *161*
30. *The Interloper* *167*
31. *At the Piano* *171*
32. *The Ghost of the Past* *173*
33. *The Dame of Athelhall* *179*
36. *The Voice* *187*
A Dream or No *189*
39. *The Walk* *193*
37. *Without Ceremony* *195*
38. *A Circular* *197*

Chapter 8 Florence Dugdale 199

34. *After the Visit* *207*
35. *On the Departure Platform* *211*
40. *A Jog-Trot Pair* *215*
41. *I Sometimes Think* *219*
42. *Nobody Comes* *221*

Chapter 9 Gertrude Bugler 223

43. *An Expostulation* *228*

Chapter 10 End Poem 231

44. *The Children and Sir Nameless* *233*

Chapter 11 Making Films 237

Author's Note 263
Acknowledgements 265
Bibliography 267
Notes 269

2
10 LOVERS 50 POEMS

FOREWORD
BY MARK DAMON CHUTTER

As Chairman and Academic Director of the Thomas Hardy Society it is a great privilege to introduce this project by Mr Giles Keating, custodian of Athelhampton House.

Thomas Hardy was a regular visitor to this Tudor Manor, starting in his teenage years when he painted a picture of the old house in watercolours, and it was here, in early August 1914, that he heard the news that Britain had declared war on Germany when a telegram was delivered to the house whilst he enjoyed supper with the Victorian owner, Alfred Cart de Lafontaine.

Hardy was, of course, an architect, a novelist and a poet and he spanned across time – a' time-torn man' – from 1840 until 1928. This collection specifically considers his relationships with women including Emma Lavinia Gifford, Florence Henniker, Tryphena Sparks, Eliza Nicholls and Florence Dugdale. In this anthology and through the associated short films we are giving voices to the poetry – by extrapolating the nuances of the verse and by aiming for a more contemporary reading of Hardy's work – to make them relevant and accessible to today's audience.

One of the special aspects about this collection is that it looks across a broad span of Hardy's love poetry, beginning with his time as a teenager and a young man, on through to the famous 1912-13 poems, and finishing with the romantic verses he wrote in his eighties.

My favourite out of the fifty poems chosen for the collection is 'The Voice,' written in the outpouring of grief after the death of his first wife Emma inspired him to return to Boscastle (where they had originally met) with Florence, who he would marry soon after. In this elegiac poem it is Emma who 'calls to me, calls to me' and there is a paradoxical emotional intensity of loss and regret and bitterness, conveyed using triplets to create the supernatural tone. Yet, Hardy does not often give the lost Emma a voice, a pattern in his poetry that can be seen in other male poets writing about their deceased wives, such as Ted Hughes's Birthday Letters (regarding his relationship with Sylvia Plath).

Furthermore, Hardy presents a narrative – a story of love, remorse, lost love, adoration and ultimately death. The women in his poetry are eclectic (such as in 'The Ruined Maid') in that they present a moment in time alongside deeper contextual issues of the period. Although I often feel that women are almost a fantasy for Hardy and rarely have an opinion or voice in his verses (even the 'She, to Him' series), everyone can read his work in a different way, and that is the wonder of great poetry.

I hope that the videos will resonate with you to offer a different lens in which to view this great writer, the women he loved and ultimately his poetry and that is how he wished to be remembered of course – as a great poet and as a 'man who used to notice such things'.

Mark Damon Chutter
Chairman and Academic Director
The Thomas Hardy Society

10 LOVERS 50 POEMS

INTRODUCTION

10 LOVERS 50 POEMS

INTRODUCTION
10 LOVERS 50 POEMS

This volume is the "book of the film" accompanying the short film series *10 Lovers 50 Poems*, which consists of some 50 videos each devoted to one poem that Thomas Hardy wrote about his most important loves.

Every video begins with its poem being read and acted by actors from the New Hardy Players, a local Dorset troupe that revives the tradition of those who performed in front of the poet himself. This is followed by interviews that discuss which lover Hardy is writing about and explore the emotional language being used. To finish, the poem is read again with its words shown on the screen. The filming took place at the Tudor house and Victorian gardens of Athelhampton where Hardy's grandfather was born, where his father restored the masonry, where his youthful romance with Phena Sparks was kindled and where he later became a regular dinner guest with his first wife Emma and his second wife Florence.

This book complements the videos, allowing readers to dwell as long as wanted on the words and giving extra background facts – and it can also be enjoyed by itself. The poems are arranged in chronological order of the events they relate to, rather than date of writing, each chapter relating to one phase of the poet's love life. Hardy wrote around five times as many poems about his first wife Emma as he did about all his other loves put together, but in this collection somewhat less than half relate to her. This re-balancing is intended to better reflect the length of the poet's life spent with Emma and allows the strength of the emotions he expresses about her to be better weighed against the very strong feelings he expresses around others.

In the main body of the book the poems are presented in full, each on a page by itself, but in this introduction short excerpts are used so as to allow an overview across all of Hardy's romantic life. Sources for the events and quotations in this introduction can be found in the detailed notes to each of the following chapters.

**

Hardy's earliest love poems are set in the country lanes of Dorset, near Athelhampton, where as a teenager he experienced his first, frustrated, loves, for Lizbie (Elizabeth Bishop) and other local "village beauties:"

Sweet Lizbie Browne
How you could smile,
How you could sing! –
How archly wile
In glance-giving,
Sweet Lizbie Browne!

But, Lizbie Browne,
I let you slip;
Shaped not a sign;
Touched never your lip
With lip of mine,
Lost Lizbie Browne!

In his late teens Hardy started studying to be an architect, which brought him to Athelhampton where his father was repairing the stonework, and he himself was helping design the new church. This was right next to the school where his cousin Phena (Tryphena) was studying. She was still too young for more than a glance or a word, but we can imagine the early stirrings of a love that was later to develop. Around this time Hardy was also working on another church, deep in the Purbeck part of Dorset, where he met Eliza Nicholls. She went away to London with a job as a lady's maid and in 1862 Hardy followed her to take up a post with a firm of architects, which was to last five years.

In London, Hardy's love-life became complicated. He proposed to Eliza and they were engaged for two or three years. This relationship ended and he briefly went out with her younger sister, Mary Jane, who was living at the family home in the country. He wrote a series of poems spoken as if in Eliza's voice. In one of them, he imagines her wanting her sibling to die:

This love puts all humanity from me;
I can but maledict her, pray her dead,
For giving love and getting love of thee –
Feeding a heart that else mine own had fed!

Hardy broke off with Mary Jane and in his final months in London in 1867, his poetry suggests that he started an affair with a famous Shakespearian actress, Mary Frances Scott-Siddons. Appropriately, he wrote about that relationship in a sonnet, the form Shakespeare uses so often:

Could that man be this I, unknowing you,
When now the knowing you is all of me,
And the old world of then is now a new,
And purpose no more what it used to be –
A thing of formal journeywork, but due
To springs that then were sealed up utterly?

But Scott-Siddons was married – and the affair ended almost as soon as it started. Hardy abandoned London in a great hurry, leaving his belongings behind in his lodgings. His official biography blames illness for this sudden move though his poems from this time exude health and happiness and it seems possible that the real reason was that the actress' military husband insisted he leave town.

Back in Dorset, Hardy re-connected with Phena who was now a young woman. He writes about their romance with great passion:

Still, I'd go the world with Beauty,
I would laugh with her and sing,
I would shun divinest duty
To resume her worshipping.
But she'd scorn my brave endeavour,
She would not balm the breeze
By murmuring "Thine for ever!"
As she did upon this leaze.

The early intensity of this relationship faded into its second year, perhaps because Phena had lost one teaching job and felt the need for greater discretion when she took up a second. Moreover, she was set for a brilliant career, which would take her to head teacher in her early 20s, but to follow that path she needed to leave Dorset to study in London. The lovers eventually each married someone else and two decades later, Phena died tragically young. Hardy mourned her in verse:

Not a line of her writing have I
Not a thread of her hair,
No mark of her late time as dame in her
dwelling, whereby
I may picture her there;
And in vain do I urge my unsight
To conceive my lost prize
At her close, whom I knew when her dreams were
upbrimming with light
And with laughter her eyes.

In early 1870, Hardy was commissioned to go to Cornwall to repair a church and he set off, lonely and miserable. In that county, which he calls by its ancient Arthurian name of Lyonnesse, he met writer Emma Gifford – and his mood changed to joy:

When I came back from Lyonnesse
With magic in my eyes,
All marked with mute surmise
My radiance rare and fathomless,
When I came back from Lyonnesse
With magic in my eyes!

A long-distance courtship lasting several years followed, and they eventually married in 1874, when Hardy was in his mid-30s. He describes a marriage that was gloriously happy at first, especially when the couple rented a cottage in a small town on the River Stour, 15 miles north of Athelhampton. His poem is actually called "A Two Year Idyll:"

Yes; such it was;
Just those two seasons unsought,
Sweeping like summertide wind on our ways;
Moving, as straws,
Hearts quick as ours in those days;

But by the 1890s, with Hardy now in his 50s, the marriage ran into trouble:

A cowled Apparition
Came pushing between;
And her notes seemed to sigh;
And the lights to burn pale,
As a spell numbed the scene.
But the maid saw no bale,
And the man no monition;
And Time laughed awry,
And the Phantom hid nigh.

The cowled apparition was Emma's growing mental illness, which Hardy writes about quite bluntly – though it's still unclear how severe this was, and whether the real issue was that the couple had drifted apart. But he had become a famous novelist, courted by society, and outwardly the couple kept up appearances, including their dinners at Athelhampton as guests of the new young owner, Alfred Cart de Lafontaine.

Yet inwardly, Hardy was deeply unhappy and in 1893, he met writer Florence Henniker, and fell in love with her. In a harsh echo of his teenage coyness with Lizbie, he didn't quite manage to kiss her:

Then the downpour ceased, to my sharp sad pain,
And the glass that had screened our forms before
Flew up, and out she sprang to her door:
I should have kissed her if the rain
Had lasted a minute more.

Miserable with Emma, he even fantasised about divorce,

A quick divorce; she will make him hers,
And I wed mine.
So Time rights all things in long, long years –
Or rather she, by her bold design!
I admire a woman no balk deters:
She has blessed my life, in fine.

But divorce was legally tricky and socially dangerous. And Florence Henniker was already married. When they went to an inn, she made clear to him that their relationship was only going to be platonic:

And we were left alone
As Love's own pair;
Yet never the love-light shone
Between us there!

So, the marriage struggled on, but Hardy hadn't given up on finding another partner. In 1905, now in his mid-60s, he met a different Florence: researcher Florence Dugdale, then in her 20s. The alliteration with three "Ls" that he uses to describe her leaves no doubt about how deeply he had fallen for her:

And I saw the large luminous living eyes
Regard me in fixed inquiring-wise

And in this new relationship, there was no hesitation about kissing:

We kissed at the barrier; and passing through
She left me, and moment by moment got
Smaller and smaller, until to my view
She was but a spot;

Florence Dugdale became a key part of Hardy's life. Initially the two of them met up in London and then in 1909 they took several trips away together. The following year, Florence introduced herself to Emma at a women's arts club in London and afterwards spent considerable time with her, even as in parallel she continued to go away and stay with Hardy himself. This arrangement continued until Emma passed away in 1912.

The way was now clear for Hardy and Florence Dugdale to marry, but first, in a great outpouring of grief, Hardy produced a series of eulogies for his late wife:

Woman much missed, how you call to me, call to me,
Saying that now you are not as you were

When you had changed from the one who was all to me,
But as at first, when our day was fair.

These poems are among the best-known of Hardy's, and feel not only moving, but also fresh and relevant. "A Circular" describes the pain of the junk mail that keeps on arriving after someone has died, as true now as it was then:

As "legal representative"
I read a missive not my own,
On new designs the senders give
For clothes, in tints as shown.

And this gay-pictured, spring-time shout
Of Fashion, hails what lady proud?
Her who before last year was out
Was costumed in a shroud.

Florence Dugdale may have been taken aback by the sheer scale of the emotional energy poured out for Hardy's deceased partner; but she was able to move in with him, and after a year's mourning had passed the couple wed early in 1914.

Their marriage was to continue for a quarter of a century until Hardy's death, and he celebrated its happy ordinariness – a stark contrast to his relationship with Emma – in the delightful poem "A Jog-Trot Pair", the rhythm of which jogs up and down like a gentle ride in a horse and cart:

Who could those common people be,
Of days the plainest, barest?
They were we;
Yes; happier than the cleverest, smartest, rarest.

Yet Hardy's final years, in the 1920s, were not completely free of romantic incidents. A troupe of actors called The Hardy Players was formed to perform dramatisations of his work, their successors appearing in the YouTube video series. One of these, Gertrude Bugler, he first saw in 1913 and a decade later he felt for her deeply enough to write:

When all we swains adore
Your featness more and more
As heroine of our artless masquings here,
And count few Wessex' daughters half so dear?

By 1924 Gertrude was married with a young baby; Hardy was keen she should play Tess in a London production and arrangements were made for babysitting. However, Florence felt that her husband's feelings were stronger than she was happy with and she asked the young actress not to go. Hardy and Gertrude never saw one another again and he died in 1928.

Neither the 10 lovers nor the 50 related poems included in this project are exhaustive; the choice aims to represent the most important relationships at each stage in Hardy's life and to show some of the strongest and clearest emotions expressed in his poetry.

INTRODUCTION

1

What do I do with this QR Code?

If you are using a smartphone you can use the camera or a QR code reader to scan the above code and link directly to the short film about the poem

If your on a computer, use your web browser and enter
www.athelhampton.com/1
Each poem that has a short-film has both a number and a QR code. If accessing via athelhampton.com simply change the number for the poem you would like to watch.

Poems without a QR code don't have a short film.

The short films are launched every fortnight starting in May 2025

10 LOVERS 50 POEMS

EARLY LOVES

10 LOVERS 50 POEMS

CHAPTER 1
EARLY LOVES

It was the "beautiful bay-red hair"[i] of "a gamekeeper's pretty daughter" that won Hardy's teenage admiration, and his poem about her, "Lizbie Browne", reads with a brisk pace mirroring the story he tells. Using 19th century language that feels inappropriate today, he says "Girls ripen fast," giving him no chance to snatch even a brief kiss before she marries someone else and disappears from his life.

The inspiration for the poem is widely believed to be Elizabeth Bishop (1837-1901).[ii] She was two and a half years older than Hardy, and it's unsurprising that she favoured someone her own age, the "best of men." He was Samuel Charles Harris, a carpenter from Berkshire, likely down in Dorset to work on railway improvements. He probably met Elizabeth through her father, who was also working in the booming train industry.

The couple didn't marry until 1860, in Fordington near Dorchester, but it's probable that Elizabeth spent a fair amount of time with her future husband in his home county before then,[iii] giving Hardy the sense of her "disappearing" some while before she decisively left Dorset for Berkshire after the wedding. She lived there with her husband for the rest of her life, having three children, the first born in her late 30s.

Another of Hardy's teenage "crushes" was Fanny Hurd, a girl at his school who sadly died young. "Retty's Phases", likely inspired by her,[iv] is about a young woman who flirts gently with the writer but dies unmarried, on her deathbed asking him to ring the bells at her funeral. The imagery entwines sensuality with death, and Hardy noted: "In many villages it was customary after the funeral of an unmarried woman to ring a peal as for her wedding while the grave was being filled in, as if Death were not to be allowed to balk her of bridal honours. Young unmarried men were always her bearers."

Alongside these and other unrequited schoolboy loves,[v] Hardy also spent time with his cousins, the Sparks sisters. They lived in Puddletown near Athelhampton, where in 1860 a new church was being built to plans drawn up by Hardy, now an apprentice architect.

The construction site adjoined the Nonconformist school where the youngest of the three sisters, Tryphena (Phena), was studying. She wasn't yet of an age for even a teenage romance, but we can imagine Hardy lifting his hat to her, kindling a relationship that was to burst into flames a few years later.

Hardy's mother, Jemima Hand, "fiercely independent and proud," lived until he was 64 and was a powerful force in his life. "A Church Romance", his imagining of how she fell for his father, uses the wonderful phrase "in her pride's despite" to capture how love overcame her instinct for independence. Perhaps Hardy is reflecting on the irony that Jemima allowed romance and desire to draw her into marriage even though she "famously"[vi] told him and his siblings not to wed, an influence that may have contributed to the failure of the two engagements described in the following chapters.

2

A CHURCH ROMANCE

(*Mellstock: circa 1835*)

She turned in the high pew, until her sight
Swept the west gallery, and caught its row
Of music-men with viol, book, and bow
Against the sinking sad tower-window light.

She turned again; and in her pride's despite
One strenuous viol's inspirer seemed to throw
A message from his string to her below,
Which said: "I claim thee as my own forthright!"

Thus their hearts' bond began, in due time signed.
And long years thence, when Age had scared Romance,
At some old attitude of his or glance
That gallery-scene would break upon her mind,
With him as minstrel, ardent, young, and trim,
Bowing "New Sabbath" or "Mount Ephraim".

3

TO LIZBIE BROWNE

I
Dear Lizbie Browne,
Where are you now?
In sun, in rain? –
Or is your brow
Past joy, past pain,
Dear Lizbie Browne?

II
Sweet Lizbie Browne,
How you could smile,
How you could sing! –
How archly wile
In glance-giving,
Sweet Lizbie Browne!

III
And, Lizbie Browne,
Who else had hair
Bay-red as yours,
Or flesh so fair
Bred out of doors,
Sweet Lizbie Browne?

10 LOVERS 50 POEMS

IV
When, Lizbie Browne,
You had just begun
To be endeared
By stealth to one,
You disappeared
My Lizbie Browne!

V
Ay, Lizbie Browne,
So swift your life,
And mine so slow,
You were a wife
Ere I could show
Love, Lizbie Browne.

VI
Still, Lizbie Browne,
You won, they said,
The best of men
When you were wed...
Where went you then,
O Lizbie Browne?

10 LOVERS 50 POEMS

VII

Dear Lizbie Browne,
I should have thought,
"Girls ripen fast,"
And coaxed and caught
You ere you passed,
Dear Lizbie Browne!

VIII

But, Lizbie Browne,
I let you slip;
Shaped not a sign;
Touched never your lip
With lip of mine,
Lost Lizbie Browne!

IX

So, Lizbie Browne,
When on a day
Men speak of me
As not, you'll say,
"And who was he?" –
Yes, Lizbie Browne!

10 LOVERS 50 POEMS

4

RETTY'S PHASES

I

Retty used to shake her head,
    Look with wicked eye;
Say, "I'd tease you, simple Ned,
    If I cared to try!"
Then she'd hot-up scarlet red,
    Stilly step away,
Much afraid that what she'd said
    Sounded bold to say.

II

Retty used to think she loved
    (Just a little) me.
Not untruly, as it proved
    Afterwards to be.
For, when weakness forced her rest
    If we walked a mile,
She would whisper she was blest
    By my clasp awhile.

10 LOVERS 50 POEMS

RETTY'S PHASES

III

Retty used at last to say
    When she neared the Vale,
"Mind that you, Dear, on that day
    Ring my wedding peal!"
And we all, with pulsing pride,
    Vigorous sounding gave
Those six bells, the while outside
    John filled in her grave.

IV

Retty used to draw me down
    To the turfy heaps,
Where, with yeoman, squire, and clown
    Noticeless she sleeps.
Now her silent slumber-place
    Seldom do I know,
For when last I saw her face
    Was so long ago!

From an old draft of 1868

10 LOVERS 50 POEMS

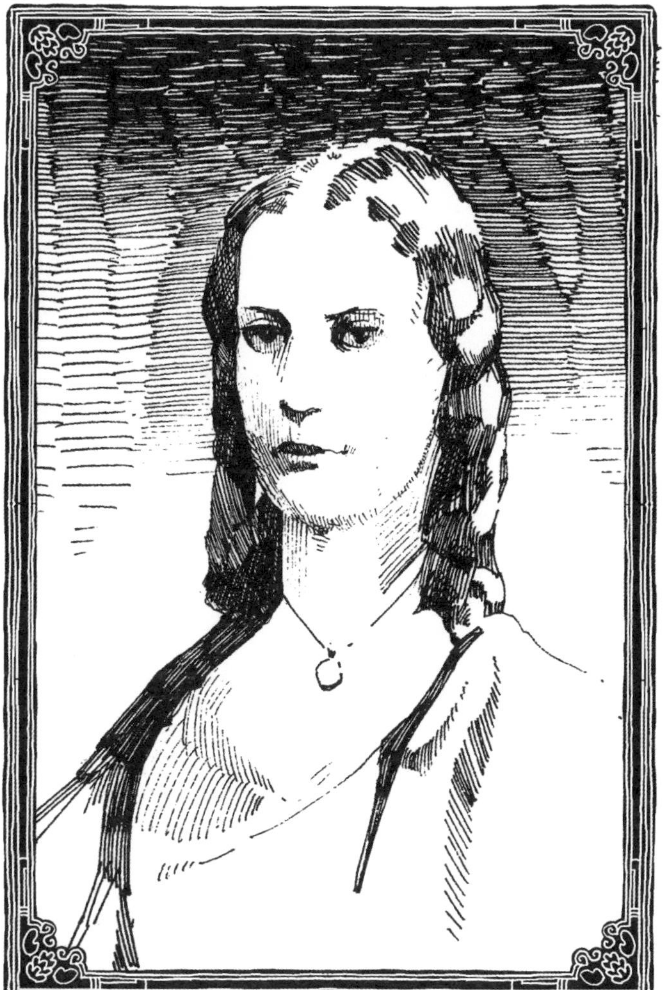

10 LOVERS 50 POEMS

CHAPTER 2
LONDON FRUSTRATIONS

In early 1861, now qualified as an architect but still living with his mother in Dorset, Hardy met Eliza Nicholls (1840-1918).[vii] Her family originated from Sussex but were spending some years in the Purbeck district of Dorset where her father, a former mariner, had been posted to a coastguard station. The eldest of seven surviving children, she had previously left home to become a lady's maid in London, periodically coming back in her holidays to see her family.

On one of those trips, she met Hardy while he was restoring a nearby church. As their friendship developed she gave him a book that he used as a diary.[viii]

With Eliza not being in Dorset very often, Hardy for a while focussed his attention on Mary Waight, who worked in a local shop, to whom he proposed early in 1862.[ix] She rejected him, being older and interested in someone else, and soon afterwards he went to London which was to be his base for half a decade.

Hardy's move allowed him to work at a thriving firm of urban architects and it also meant he could be near Eliza, for shortly after arriving he changed lodgings to a location close to her in Paddington. As he courted her, he started to observe a side of London life that he could never have seen from Dorset – the financial and emotional dilemma faced by most young women from the country, like Eliza. He wrote about this in the witty, flowing music-hall style[xiii] of "The Ruined Maid," which contains a deadly attack on Victorian social mores.

In the poem, a young woman from the country, up in London for a visit, meets an old friend who wears fine clothes and has smooth skin and explains proudly that she is "ruined" – a contemporary expression meaning that she is obtaining money from a man or men in return for sexual services. Hardy is highlighting the hypocrisy of Victorian society, which generally offered poorly educated young rural women only one way to obtain a substantial income, and then applied a pejorative term when they choose to use it. He mocks this double standard by having Melia express pride in the description applied to her. He would have been aware that Eliza's income as a lady's maid in London would have been higher than she could have made in Dorset, but considerably less than she might have aspired to had she been "ruined."

"From Her in the Country" touches the same theme in a different way. It is written in the voice of a young woman from the countryside. She spends the first two stanzas of this lovely sonnet (in Shakespearian form, its line-ending rhymes within but not between verses) extolling the nature around her, comparing it favourably with urban life. Hardy chooses words to emphasise this; the alliterative "crass clanging town" has a slightly unpleasant grinding feel that contrasts with the softness of "One little bud." But in the third stanza, her certainty is starting to break, and in the final rhyming couplet there is an unequivocal and sharp change of tone (volta) as she longs to move to the wonderfully resonant "city din and sin."

After some time in London, Hardy proposed to Eliza and was accepted. The engagement continued some years, even after she moved away from London, first to a new job in Surrey and then to spend time with her parents who had returned to their original home village in Sussex. He travelled to see her there fairly often and wrote about her in "The Musing Maiden".[xii]

The opening "Why so often, silent one,/Do you steal away alone?" can be interpreted as Hardy suggesting to Eliza that being apart frequently is straining the relationship. And the lines in the closing stanza "To mark the moon was our delight;/Up there our eyesights touch at will" feel romantic rather than sensual when compared with phrases like our ecstasy used in some of Hardy's later love poems.

By 1866 the relationship had shattered irrevocably. That year Hardy wrote a series of four poems about the break-up, beginning with "She to Him I." They are written in Eliza's voice, describing her emotions as he perceives them.[xi] The first poem of the series has a plaintive tone, expressing the hope that she can at least be friends with Hardy in the distant future: "Will you not grant to old affection's claim/The hand of friendship down Life's sunless hill?"

One obvious interpretation is that Hardy understood that Eliza felt abandoned and is showing impressive self-awareness in articulating the pain she endured. But another possibility is that this poem is a vehicle for Hardy's own frustration and anger, even that he purposefully projects emotions of loss onto Eliza that go beyond what he believed her to be feeling. In the notebooks he wrote at this time he uses imagery that signals the intensity of his sexual feelings and perhaps he'd been dissatisfied by this aspect of the relationship; maybe he felt that the exceptionally religious Eliza was imposing restrictions on the couple's physical life together that went beyond what was needed to avoid pregnancy.

Hardy's sense of romantic failure, exacerbated by the rejection of his poetry by publishers, seems to well up in the sonnet "Hap". This brilliant, angry cry at the sheer arbitrariness of bad luck culminates in the final couplet "These purblind Doomsters had as readily strown/Blisses about my pilgrimage as pain."

During his visits to Eliza's family home in Sussex, Hardy had met her younger sister, Mary Jane Nicholls (1845-1877). He started to go with her, probably in 1866 as his relationship with Eliza ended.[x] This romance does not seem to have lasted long, possibly about a year or so, perhaps less,[xvi] but he celebrates it in "Her Definition", a charming poem about writing a poem. Written in summer 1866,[xvii] this describes the poet's search for suitable words to describe his love. He realises that he can honour her with the simplest of phrases, "maiden mine," in the same way that very valuable objects may be carried in "common chests."

Hardy writes about Eliza's reaction to his relationship with Mary Jane in "She to Him IV". The tone is of bitter anger, directed at her sister, who she hopes will die: "This love puts all humanity from me;/I can but maledict her, pray her dead." As with the earlier "She, to Him" poems, there are alternative ways to interpret this. It could be seen as Hardy perceptively understanding the pain he has caused his ex-fiancee. Or, it might be viewed as a selfish piece in which by portraying his ex-lover as a heartless woman capable of wishing her sibling dead, he blunts the pain he himself feels at being no longer engaged to her.

Mary Jane, after she stopped seeing Hardy, courted with Harry Beach, who lived in her village in Sussex and had risen from being a groom and then a decorator's assistant to become a waterworks inspector. He was a decade older than her and his first wife had died young, perhaps in childbirth. They wed in the local church Sussex in July 1869 and went to live in Brighton, but sadly she died from a tumour in the uterus aged just 32 in 1877[xv] and there are no records of any live-born children.

Meanwhile Eliza, after her engagement to Hardy had ended, continued her career as a lady's maid into her 30s, working for some time in Christchurch. Then after her mother died in 1878 she moved back to live with her father permanently, likely helping him to run the pub in their home village that he'd taken on after retiring from the coastguard.

After he passed in 1906, she moved in with her brother and his wife in Hove. She never married, and she wrote to Hardy after his first wife died and he invited her to visit him.[xiv] Some biographers see this as consistent with a literal interpretation of the "She, to Him" poems as portrayals of a sad and frustrated woman, who would always hark back to her time with Hardy. But she is described in the 1911 census as having "private means" and when she died in 1918, she left bequests totalling £893, worth somewhere between £90,000 and £800,000 in today's money.[xv] This suggests an alternative view, of Eliza as an empowered woman who had achieved independence in a man's world through her hard work, with Hardy's poems about her being vehicles for his own feelings rather than literal descriptions of hers.

Hardy, after his relationships with the Nicholls sisters had ended, spent one more year in the capital – and his romantic fortunes were to change sharply for the better.

LONDON FRUSTRATIONS

5

THE RUINED MAID

"O 'Melia, my dear, this does everything crown!
Who could have supposed I should meet you in Town?
And whence such fair garments, such prosperi-ty?"
–"O didn't you know I'd been ruined?" said she.

– "You left us in tatters, without shoes or socks,
Tired of digging potatoes, and spudding up docks;
And now you've gay bracelets and bright feathers three!" –
"Yes: that's how we dress when we're ruined," said she.

– "At home in the barton you said 'thee' and 'thou',
And 'thik oon', and 'theäs oon', and 't'other'; but now
Your talking quite fits 'ee for high compa-ny!" –
"Some polish is gained with one's ruin," said she.

10 LOVERS 50 POEMS

THE RUINED MAID

– "Your hands were like paws then, your face blue
                                        and bleak
But now I'm bewitched by your delicate cheek,
And your little gloves fit as on any la-dy!" –
"We never do work when we're ruined," said she.

– "You used to call home-life a hag-ridden dream,
And you'd sigh, and you'd sock; but at present you
                                          seem
To know not of megrims or melancho-ly!" –
"True. One's pretty lively when ruined," said she.

– "I wish I had feathers, a fine sweeping gown,
And a delicate face, and could strut about Town!" –
"My dear – a raw country girl, such as you be,
Cannot quite expect that. You ain't ruined," said
                                                                she.

Westbourne Park Villas, 1866

6

FROM HER IN THE COUNTRY

I thought and thought of thy crass clanging town
To folly, till convinced such dreams were ill,
I held my heart in bond, and tethered down
Fancy to where I was, by force of will.

I said: How beautiful are these flowers, this wood,
One little bud is far more sweet to me
Than all man's urban shows; and then I stood
Urging new zest for bird, and bush, and tree;

And strove to feel my nature brought it forth
Of instinct, or no rural maid was I;
But it was vain; for I could not see worth
Enough around to charm a midge or fly,

And mused again on city din and sin,
Longing to madness I might move therein!

16 W.P.V., 1866

7

SHE, TO HIM. I

When you shall see me in the toils of Time,
My lauded beauties carried off from me,
My eyes no longer stars as in their prime,
My name forgot of Maiden Fair and Free;

When, in your being, heart concedes to mind,
And judgment, though you scarce its process know,
Recalls the excellencies I once enshrined,
And you are irked that they have withered so:

Remembering mine the loss is, not the blame,
That Sportsman Time but rears his brood to kill,
Knowing me in my soul the very same –
One who would die to spare you touch of ill! –
Will you not grant to old affection's claim
The hand of friendship down Life's sunless hill?

1866

10 LOVERS 50 POEMS

THE MUSING MAIDEN

"Why so often, silent one,
Do you steal away alone?"
Starting, half she turned her head,
    And guiltily she said: –

"When the vane points to his far town
I go upon the hog-backed down,
And think the breeze that stroked his lip
    Over my own may slip.

When he walks at close of day
I ramble on the white highway,
And think it reaches to his feet:
    A meditation sweet!

10 LOVERS 50 POEMS

When coasters hence to London sail
I watch their puffed wings waning pale;
His window opens near the quay;
    Their coming he can see.

I go to meet the moon at night;
To mark the moon was our delight;
Up there our eyesights touch at will
    If such he practise still".

W.P.V. October 1866 (recopied)

8

HAP

If but some vengeful god would call to me
From up the sky, and laugh: "Thou suffering thing,
Know that thy sorrow is my ecstasy,
That thy love's loss is my hate's profiting!"

Then would I bear it, clench myself, and die,
Steeled by the sense of ire unmerited;
Half-eased in that a Powerfuller than I
Had willed and meted me the tears I shed.

But not so. How arrives it joy lies slain,
And why unblooms the best hope ever sown?
– Crass Casualty obstructs the sun and rain,
And dicing Time for gladness casts a moan. . . .
These purblind Doomsters had as readily strown
Blisses about my pilgrimage as pain.

1866

10 LOVERS 50 POEMS

LONDON FRUSTRATION

9

HER DEFINITION

I lingered through the night to break of day,
Nor once did sleep extend a wing to me,
Intently busied with a vast array
Of epithets that should outfigure thee.

Full-featured terms – all fitless – hastened by,
And this sole speech remained: "That maiden
mine!" –
Debarred from due description then did I
Perceive the indefinite phrase could yet define.

As common chests encasing wares of price
Are borne with tenderness through halls of state,
For what they cover, so the poor device
Of homely wording I could tolerate,
Knowing its unadornment held as freight
The sweetest image outside Paradise.

W.P.V., Summer: 1866

10

SHE, TO HIM, IV

This love puts all humanity from me;
I can but maledict her, pray her dead,
For giving love and getting love of thee –
Feeding a heart that else mine own had fed!

How much I love I know not, life not known,
Save as one unit I would add love by;
But this I know, my being is but thine own –
Fused from its separateness by ecstasy.

And thus I grasp thy amplitudes, of her
Ungrasped, though helped by nigh-regarding eyes;
Canst thou then hate me as an envier
Who see unrecked what I so dearly prize?
Believe me, Lost One, Love is lovelier
The more it shapes its moan in selfish-wise.

1866

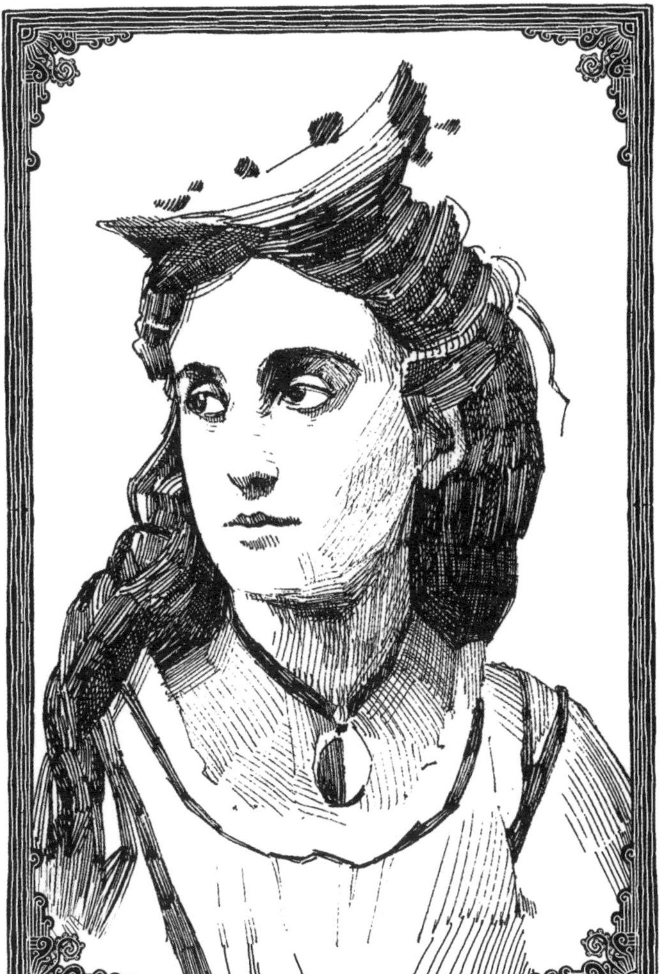

10 LOVERS 50 POEMS

CHAPTER 3
LONDON CLIMAX

During Hardy's final few months in London in 1867, he penned a trio of poems whose tone is utterly different from the previous year's outpouring of frustration.

He writes joyously about Mary Frances Scott-Siddons, whose impressive career had began two years before he met her, with her appearance on stage in Nottingham as Portia at the age of 21. Hardy saw her play Rosalind in a West End performance of *As You Like It*, a fortnight into a run that was to last for eight months and be met with critical acclaim.

Hardy describes her acting in the sonnet "To an Impersonator of Rosalind" and leaves no doubt who it refers to, by dating it Sunday 21st April 1867 and indicating that he wrote it in his office at 8 Adelphi Terrace, a short walk from the Haymarket Theatre where she had performed the night before.[xx] The poem asks whether Shakespeare himself might have looked forward in time and been inspired by seeing the "soft sweet mien" of her portrayal of Rosalind.

Five years earlier, she had married a Royal Naval officer who was, or became, an alcoholic and from whom she later separated. If her marriage was already going wrong in 1867, she might have been interested in a relationship with someone else; and for Hardy, she would have had the attraction of being a married woman who might offer a break from his earlier frustrations. His next poem, "To an Actress", is a celebration, with no hint of the jealousy and rejection seen in the 1866 poems. It has a sensuality not seen in any of his poems about Eliza or Mary Jane: the opening up of "springs" that had previously been "sealed up utterly." A clear interpretation is that Hardy had found a partner more emotionally and physically responsive than the young women from the country he had written about before.

There is no reference to a romance with Mary Frances in the official (auto) biography – and it is the same for Eliza, Mary Jane and Phena. Hardy chose to write about his feelings for all of these women in the flowing and ambiguous medium of poetry rather than the bluntness of prose. In the case of the other three, the evidence from the poems was subsequently corroborated by oral histories recorded by their relatives, and over the years the research community has come to accept that Hardy had some form of relationship with them. There are no similar sources relating to Mary Frances. So, it is up to readers to form their own judgement on whether this was a fantasy or a real relationship – based on the poetry alone.

The final poem in this chapter is the unusual and delightful poem "1967" in which Hardy looks forward a century to an era more enlightened than his own: "In five score summers.../A scope above this blinkered time". He obviously didn't know that a hundred years ahead London would be headed for the more socially liberal, though imperfect, Swinging Sixties. But he observed the narrowness of the society around him and predicted that things would get better. Given when this poem was written, it may well be that Mary Frances is the "dear" referred to.

In late July 1867, Hardy went back to Dorset, leaving his books and other belongings behind in his lodgings. In his official (auto) biography, the reason given is a long-term weakening of health from the stenches in London and a poor lifestyle spent largely indoors, the final spur being news of a job available at his former employer in Dorchester.

This account is difficult to reconcile with the ecstatic tone of the poems about Mary Frances, radiating energy and happiness, written just three months earlier. One possible explanation is that Hardy's relationship with Mary Frances had been discovered by her husband and he had to leave town quickly – and that, rather than reveal this, the biography over-emphasises the health issue.

Mary Frances' acting career continued for another twelve years and included two tours in the USA and one in Australia.[xxi] She briefly took on the role of manager at the Haymarket Theatre, a notable achievement for a woman in Victorian England whose parents and spouse were not from the industry. She then had a second career as a reader of plays in locations including the USA and Germany, where she read to the Emperor and his wife. She passed away in her early 50s in 1896.[xxii]

11

TO AN IMPERSONATOR OF ROSALIND

Did he who drew her in the years ago –
Till now conceived creator of her grace –
With telescopic sight high natures know,
Discern remote in Time's untravelled space

Your soft sweet mien, your gestures, as do we,
And with a copyist's hand but set them down,
Glowing yet more to dream our ecstasy
When his Original should be forthshown?

For, kindled by that animated eye,
Whereto all fairnesses about thee brim,
And by thy tender tones, what wight can fly
The wild conviction welling up in him

That he at length beholds woo, parley, plead,
The "very, very Rosalind" indeed!

8 Adelphi Terrace, 21 April 1867

12

TO AN ACTRESS

I read your name when you were strange to me,
Where it stood blazoned bold with many more;
I passed it vacantly, and did not see
Any great glory in the shape it wore.

O cruelty, the insight barred me then!
Why did I not possess me with its sound,
And in its cadence catch and catch again
Your nature's essence floating therearound?

Could *that* man be this I, unknowing you,
When now the knowing you is all of me,
And the old world of then is now a new,
And purpose no more what it used to be –
A thing of formal journeywork, but due
To springs that then were sealed up utterly?

1867

13

1967

In five-score summers! All new eyes,
New minds, new modes, new fools, new wise;
New woes to weep, new joys to prize;

With nothing left of me and you
In that live century's vivid view
Beyond a pinch of dust or two;

A century which, if not sublime,
Will show, I doubt not, at its prime,
A scope above this blinkered time.

– Yet what to me how far above?
For I would only ask thereof
That thy worm should be my worm, Love!

16 Westbourne Park Villas, 1867

10 LOVERS 50 POEMS

PHENA

10 LOVERS 50 POEMS

CHAPTER 4
PHENA

When Hardy arrived back in Dorset in July 1867, his cousin Phena had moved from the Nonconformist school at Athelhampton[xxiii] to the Church of England school in nearby Puddletown. There, she worked as a pupil-teacher – a role in which she taught young children while continuing her own education. She was aged 16 and had grown into a beautiful young woman. Hardy fell deeply in love with her, according to her daughter Nellie.[xxiv]

Many of the fields near the school were "eweleaze", meaning they were left unploughed for sheep to graze on. Hardy describes the couple's passion together in his poem "In a Eweleaze near Weatherbury": "With one who kindled gaily/Love's fitful ecstasies!" Though written years later, after Phena's untimely death and containing reflections on ageing and the passage of time, this nonetheless exudes the happiness of a young couple together in the warmth of a field away from the village.

Two other poems also look back to those warm and happy days together, emphasising the intensity of the passion and its hidden nature. These words are from "At Rushy Pond": "I had called a woman to me/From across this water, ardently" while these are from "A Spot", with wonderful alliterations in both lines: "Two sat here, transport-tossed,/Lit by a living love".

"The Place on the Map" also resonates with physical intimacy, telling of how for "weeks and weeks we had loved beneath that blazing blue." But there is a twist in this poem, in the form of the sudden revelation of an unplanned pregnancy, and the penalties that society would impose because of it: "...she told what.../in realms of reason would have joyed our double soul/Wore a torrid tragic light/ Under order-keeping's rigorous control."

There are no official records of a baby born to Phena and Hardy, so this might refer to the conception of a baby subsequently given to others to be brought up, or to a false alarm, or a pregnancy that miscarried. Alternatively, some researchers believe it describes the summer three years later at the start of Hardy's courtship of Emma, while others suggest it is about a child fathered by his friend Henry Moule.[xxv]

In January 1868, Phena abruptly lost her job at Puddletown school, even though it was the middle of the academic year. This was an especially strict Church of England school and it seems that Phena had been asked to leave because of the love affair.[xxvi] The local network of Nonconformists based at Athelhampton rallied around to save her career, finding her a replacement post at their school a few miles away at Coryates near Weymouth, which she took up in Autumn 1868 at the start of the new school year.[xxvii]

Phena would have been anxious to avoid rekindling the scandal in her new job and the intense phase of the relationship faded, as described by Hardy in his 1869 poem "Her Initials".[ixxviii] The simple form of two quatrains (four-line stanzas) belies its power, with the image of light, which can be understood to represent passion, running through it – the obscure word "effulgent" meaning "shining brightly." The first stanza, in the past tense, talks of Hardy's "rapture" and describes him writing his love's initials. In contrast the second stanza, in present tense, describes how "...the radiance has waned away!"

"Her Initials" is a poem about the ending or fading of a relationship yet its tone is in complete contrast to Hardy's poetry about his break-up with Eliza, notably the "She, to Him" sequence. It celebrates the bright happiness of the past and is sad about its passing, but has none of the bitter resentment of those earlier verses.

The break-up has been described as "an ambiguous parting, with fluctuating emotions".[xxix] Reflecting this, in June 1869 Hardy moved to Weymouth which brought him closer to Phena – but also to the seaside dance halls where he could easily meet other women. This equivocal late phase in the relationship finished in late January 1870, when Phena left Dorset to start her long wished-for studies at a major teacher training college in London. Hardy carefully noted the starting date of her course in his Bible, knowing she was to live in convent-like conditions for two years, bringing any vestiges of their earlier passions to a clear end.[xxxi]

Hardy marked the break by returning from his Weymouth lodgings to his family home near Dorchester. This was a convenient location for seeing Cassie Pole, whom he had probably met in the seaside dance halls on her days off and who worked barely a mile away.[xxxii] But a month later when he went to Cornwall he was still "lonesome" (see "When I Set Out for Lyonnesse" in the next chapter), suggesting that whoever he may have met recently, his emotions on the journey that would lead him to his first wife Emma Gifford were dominated by the final break-up of his passionate relationship with Phena.

After Phena qualified in late 1871 she was appointed headmistress of Plymouth Day School, a remarkable achievement at age 20. The chair of the interview panel remarked that she was very young. She replied "Well sir, that is a thing that time will cure".[xxxiii] The following year she met Charles Frederick Gale; they married in 1877 and had four children.

Tragically, Phena died on 17th March 1890, aged just 38. By that time, Hardy had been married to Emma for nearly two decades, though his relationship with her had become strained. On a train journey in early March 1890, he wrote the first stanza of a poem with first line "Not a line of her writing have I". In his journal afterwards he wrote: "Curious instance of sympathetic telepathy. The woman whom I was thinking of, a cousin, was dying at the time and I quite in ignorance of it, she died six days later. The remainder of the piece not written until after her death."

The poem that resulted was "Thoughts of Phena, at News of Her Death". It is rare for Hardy to mention someone's real name in the title of a poem, so this seems an indication of how important she was to him.[xxxiv]

He evokes her loss with a nagging repetition of negation at the poem's start: "Not a line of her writing have I/Not a thread of her hair/No mark of her late time". This repetition, like a keening lament, resumes in parallel lines at the poem's end.

Hardy illustrated this poem with a picture of his dead love imagined as lying on the couch in the living-room of Max Gate, the house he had built for himself and Emma and where they were living at that time. The body is wrapped in a shroud with no features visible, true to the spirit of the poem.

In July 1890, accompanied by his brother Henry, Hardy visited the Gales' house where he met Phena's children. Her eldest daughter Nellie describes what happened on that hot day when she came home: "Hardy and his brother Henry were in the parlour. [My father] stayed in the pantry cutting bread… [saying] "I don't want to see Hardy, you entertain him." Served lunch of ham. My father was coldly polite and Tom was formal as well. I knew there was friction there."[xxxv]

After this visit, Hardy wrote "To an Orphan Child" (corrected to "To a Motherless Child" in later publications). This is another poem that exudes Hardy's passion for Phena, which it does in a most unusual and unsettling way, by wishing that her youngest child could have only her genes and thus be a kind of re-incarnation of her.

14

IN A EWELEAZE NEAR WEATHERBURY

The years have gathered grayly
    Since I danced upon this leaze
With one who kindled gaily
    Love's fitful ecstasies!
But despite the term as teacher,
    I remain what I was then
In each essential feature
    Of the fantasies of men.

Yet I note the little chisel
    Of never-napping Time
Defacing wan and grizzel
    The blazon of my prime.
When at night he thinks me sleeping
    I feel him boring sly
Within my bones, and heaping
    Quaintest pains for by-and-by.

10 LOVERS 50 POEMS

Still, I'd go the world with Beauty,
    I would laugh with her and sing,
I would shun divinest duty
    To resume her worshipping.
But she'd scorn my brave endeavour,
    She would not balm the breeze
By murmuring "Thine for ever!"
    As she did upon this leaze.

10 LOVERS 50 POEMS

AT RUSHY-POND

On the frigid face of the heath-hemmed pond
    There shaped the half-grown moon:
Winged whiffs from the north with a husky croon
    Blew over and beyond.

And the wind flapped the moon in its float on the pool,
    And stretched it to oval form;
Then corkscrewed it like a wriggling worm;
    Then wanned it weariful.

And I cared not for conning the sky above
    Where hung the substant thing,
For my thought was earthward sojourning
    On the scene I had vision of.

Since there it was once, in a secret year,
    I had called a woman to me
From across this water, ardently –
    And practised to keep her near;

10 LOVERS 50 POEMS

AT RUSHY-POND

Till the last weak love-words had been said,
    And ended was her time,
And blurred the bloomage of her prime,
    And white the earlier red.

And the troubled orb in the pond's sad shine
    Was her very wraith, as scanned
When she withdrew thence, mirrored, and
    Her days dropped out of mine.

15

A SPOT

In years defaced and lost,
Two sat here, transport-tossed,
Lit by a living love
The wilted world knew nothing of:
    Scared momently
    By gaingivings,
    Then hoping things
    That could not be...

Of love and us no trace
Abides upon the place;
The sun and shadows wheel,
Season and season sereward steal;
    Foul days and fair
    Here, too, prevail,
    And gust and gale
    As everywhere.

10 LOVERS 50 POEMS

But lonely shepherd souls
Who bask amid these knolls
May catch a faery sound
On sleepy noontides from the ground:
    "O not again
    Till Earth outwears
    Shall love like theirs
    Suffuse this glen!"

THE PLACE ON THE MAP

I

I look upon the map that hangs by me –
Its shires and towns and rivers lined in
                              varnished artistry –
  And I mark a jutting height
Coloured purple, with a margin of blue sea.

II

– 'Twas a day of latter summer, hot and dry;
Ay, even the waves seemed drying as we
                              walked on, she and I,
  By this spot where, calmly quite,
She unfolded what would happen by and by.

III

This hanging map depicts the coast and place,
And re-creates therewith our unforeboded
                              troublous case
  All distinctly to my sight,
And her tension, and the aspect of her face.

10 LOVERS 50 POEMS

IV

Weeks and weeks we had loved beneath that
                              blazing blue,
Which had lost the art of raining, as her eyes to-
                              day had too,
   While she told what, as by sleight,
Shot our firmament with rays of ruddy hue.

V

   For the wonder and the wormwood of the whole
Was that what in realms of reason would have
                              joyed our double soul
   Wore a torrid tragic light
Under order-keeping's rigorous control.

VI

   So, the map revives her words, the spot, the time,
And the thing we found we had to face before
                              the next year's prime;
   The charted coast stares bright,
And its episode comes back in pantomime.

10 LOVERS 50 POEMS

HER INITIALS

Upon a poet's page I wrote
Of old two letters of her name;
Part seemed she of the effulgent thought
Whence that high singer's rapture came.

–When now I turn the leaf the same
Immortal light illumes the lay,
But from the letters of her name
The radiance has waned away!

1869

16

THOUGHTS OF PHENA
AT NEWS OF HER DEATH

Not a line of her writing have I,
    Not a thread of her hair,
No mark of her late time as dame in her
                  dwelling, whereby
    I may picture her there;
    And in vain do I urge my unsight
        To conceive my lost prize
At her close, whom I knew when her dreams
              were upbrimming with light,
    And with laughter her eyes.

    What scenes spread around her last days,
        Sad, shining, or dim?
Did her gifts and compassions enray and
                enarch her sweet ways
        With an aureate nimb?
    Or did life-light decline from her years,
        And mischances control
Her full day-star; unease, or regret, or
              forebodings, or fears
        Disennoble her soul?

10 LOVERS 50 POEMS

THOUGHTS OF PHENA AT NEWS OF HER DEATH

    Thus I do but the phantom retain
        Of the maiden of yore
As my relic; yet haply the best of her – fined in
                            my brain
        It may be the more
    That no line of her writing have I,
        Nor a thread of her hair,
No mark of her late time as dame in her
                        dwelling, whereby
        I may picture her there.

March 1890

17

TO A MOTHERLESS CHILD

Ah, child, thou art but half thy darling mother's;
    Hers couldst thou wholly be,
My light in thee would outglow all in others;
    She would relive to me.
But niggard Nature's trick of birth
    Bars, lest she overjoy,
Renewal of the loved on earth
    Save with alloy.

The Dame has no regard, alas, my maiden,
    For love and loss like mine –
No sympathy with mindsight memory-laden;
    Only with fickle eyne.
To her mechanic artistry
    My dreams are all unknown,
And why I wish that thou couldst be
    But One's alone!

10 LOVERS 50 POEMS

EMMA - EARLY HAPPINESS

10 LOVERS 50 POEMS

CHAPTER 5
EMMA - EARLY HAPPINESS

In early 1870, his love affair with Phena now finished, Hardy was sent to Cornwall to survey a parish church for repairs. It was a slow journey of over 100 miles, starting with a long walk to the distant Great Western station in Dorchester and involving four trains and a cart journey. For Hardy, this was much more than a long railway ride; he describes it in "When I set Out for Lyonnesse" as a profound emotional journey.

He began it by plodding to the station before dawn as a single man "And starlight lit my lonesomeness." He ended it deeply in love: "With magic in my eyes."

The new romance was with Emma Gifford (1840-1912), who lived in the rectory attached to the church he was to restore, as sister of the rector's wife.

Although Emma's family had suffered financial loss, by living with her sibling she did not have to work, and had time to experiment with writing and to develop impressive equestrian skills: "The moment she was on a horse she was part of the animal".[xxxvi] Later in life her poetry appeared in mass-circulation journals and her work on the role women could play in government, published in a leading radical magazine, still feels relevant to today's gender politics.

Hardy and Emma began a long-distance courtship that was to last for over three years. The light-hearted gaiety of "Great Things" captures the happiness of Hardy's mood at this time: taking a glass of cider at the pub in Upwey near Weymouth, and dancing, just as its words seem to do with their internal rhymes in the third lines of each stanza.

Almost all of Hardy's poems about Emma were written after her death and exude melancholy, often emphasised by starting with joy but ending in sadness. In "Beeny Cliff", the rhyming triplets tell a flowing story that begins: "And the woman riding high above with bright hair flapping free –/The woman whom I loved so, and who loyally loved me", but move on to a grimmer reality: "The woman now is – elsewhere." There is a similar transition in "The Phantom Horsewoman", from a "sweet soft scene.../Warm, real, and keen", to a "ghost-girl-rider". But "Lyonnesse" is a remarkable exception to this pattern. Despite also being written after Emma's passing, it follows the opposite path, beginning with the poet's lonesome misery and ending in the radiance of love; while "Great Things" is happy throughout.

Hardy's crucial first trip to Cornwall had lasted just three days; his next trip was five months later and lasted for three summer weeks. A month or so later he wrote Emma's initials in his Bible beside these lines: "Thy lips are like a thread of scarlet.../Thy two breasts are like two young roes that are twins" (from 'The Song of Solomon'), a sensual message echoing the physical passion manifest in his poems about Phena.[xxxvii] The intensity of that summer with

Emma was such that Hardy's (auto) biography states that by the autumn he felt "virtually if not distinctly engaged".xxxviii

The couple's distance dating continued for another two years. Hardy made only five more visits to Cornwall, but they got together in Bath for nearly two weeks in mid 1873 and by the end of that year Emma had moved out of the rectory and come to London.

Meanwhile, Hardy's writing career developed, with modest success for *A Pair of Blue Eyes*, a novel based on his relationship with Emma and featuring an imaginary manor with architecture inspired by Athelhampton's, and then from late 1873, *Far From the Madding Crowd* was published in serialised form, sealing his reputation as a writer.

This success allowed the couple to marry in London in September 1874. After a honeymoon in France, the newlyweds lived in London, followed by short stints in Yeovil and Swanage. Hardy's poem about a trip to Bournemouth just a year after their nuptials, "We Sat At the Window", suggests that the marriage was not living up to the romance of their courtship. The couple, trapped indoors by heavy rain onomatopoeically captured as "Each gutter and spout/Babbled unchecked", are unable to see how much the other has to offer.

Then, happiness returned, when from 1876 to 1878 they took a two-year lease on a cottage in Sturminster Newton, in the middle of Dorset. In "On Sturminster Footbridge", the criss-cross patterns like scales on a snake ("reticulations") at the beginning are in the inanimate water, but by the end they have become human in the form of Emma, glowing in the darkness like a "lattice-gleam".

This poem also has another of the rare allusions in Hardy's numerous verses about Emma that can be read as a direct reference to their sexual life together. The wonderful final alliteration "when midnight moans" captures the sensuousness of a phase in their lives when the couple were hoping for a baby.[xxxix]

The happiness of that time is also described in the title of "Two Year Idyll" and in its evocative first-stanza phrases: "Sweeping like summertide wind" and "Hearts quick as ours". But this poem was written long after those years at Sturminster, and its final stanza emphasises that the joy was to end once the lease ran out: "Nothing came after."

"Overlooking the River Stour" approaches the same theme in a different way. Initially the poem describes Hardy's enjoyment of the nature at Sturminster, and he strengthens this message in each stanza by making the second and closing line-pairs the same. But in the final stanza, those line-pairs differ subtly from one another, emphasising that there is a volta (stark change of emotional tone) to self-recrimination, as he "...let, alack,/These less things hold my gaze!"

In "The Musical Box" there is again a tension between the happiness at Sturminster and Hardy's failure to make it last, but there is no single volta, rather a repeated intertwining of upbeat phrases like "the fair colour of the time" with darker, unheeded warnings. And halfway through, there is a lovely image of Emma "white-muslined" which seems to epitomise the joyful early days of marriage. A stark contrast with the photos of an older Emma always dressed in black – and a harbinger of the "white spot of muslin" that Hardy was to use to describe Florence Dugdale four decades later.

18

WHEN I SET OUT FOR LYONNESSE

When I set out for Lyonnesse,
    A hundred miles away,
    The rime was on the spray,
And starlight lit my lonesomeness
When I set out for Lyonnesse
    A hundred miles away.

What would bechance at Lyonnesse
    While I should sojourn there
    No prophet durst declare,
Nor did the wisest wizard guess
What would bechance at Lyonnesse
    While I should sojourn there.

When I came back from Lyonnesse
    With magic in my eyes,
    All marked with mute surmise
My radiance rare and fathomless,
When I came back from Lyonnesse
    With magic in my eyes!

1870

19

GREAT THINGS

Sweet cyder is a great thing,
    A great thing to me,
Spinning down to Weymouth town
    By Ridgway thirstily,
And maid and mistress summoning
    Who tend the hostelry:
O cyder is a great thing,
    A great thing to me!

The dance it is a great thing,
    A great thing to me,
With candles lit and partners fit
    For night-long revelry;
And going home when day-dawning
    Peeps pale upon the lea:
O dancing is a great thing,
    A great thing to me!

10 LOVERS 50 POEMS

Love is, yea, a great thing,
    A great thing to me,
When, having drawn across the lawn
    In darkness silently,
A figure flits like one a-wing
    Out from the nearest tree:
O love is, yes, a great thing,
    A great thing to me!

Will these be always great things,
    Great things to me? . . .
Let it befall that One will call,
    'Soul, I have need of thee:'
What then? Joy-jaunts, impassioned flings,
    Love, and its ecstasy,
Will always have been great things,
    Great things to me!

20

BEENY CLIFF

I

O the opal and the sapphire of that wandering
                                      western sea,
And the woman riding high above with bright
                                      hair flapping free –
The woman whom I loved so, and who loyally
                                      loved me.

II

The pale mews plained below us, and the
                                      waves seemed far away
In a nether sky, engrossed in saying their
                                      ceaseless babbling say,
As we laughed light-heartedly aloft on that
                                      clear-sunned March day.

III

A little cloud then cloaked us, and there flew
                                      an irised rain,
And the Atlantic dyed its levels with a dull
                                      misfeatured stain,
And then the sun burst out again, and purples
                                      prinked the main.

10 LOVERS 50 POEMS

IV

– Still in all its chasmal beauty bulks old Beeny
                                        to the sky,
And shall she and I not go there once again
                                        now March is nigh,
And the sweet things said in that March say
                                        anew there by and by?

V

What if still in chasmal beauty looms that wild
                                        weird western shore,
The woman now is – elsewhere – whom the
                                        ambling pony bore,
And nor knows nor cares for Beeny, and will
                                        laugh there nevermore.

March 1870 - March 1913

10 LOVERS 50 POEMS

THE PHANTOM HORSEWOMAN

I

Queer are the ways of a man I know:
    He comes and stands
    In a careworn craze,
    And looks at the sands
    And the seaward haze
    With moveless hands
    And face and gaze,
    Then turns to go . . .
And what does he see when he gazes so?

II

They say he sees as an instant thing
    More clear than to-day,
    A sweet soft scene
    That was once in play
    By that briny green;
    Yes, notes alway
    Warm, real, and keen,
    What his back years bring –
A phantom of his own figuring.

10 LOVERS 50 POEMS

III

Of this vision of his they might say more:
    Not only there
    Does he see this sight,
    But everywhere
    In his brain – day, night,
    As if on the air
    It were drawn rose bright –
    Yea, far from that shore
Does he carry this vision of heretofore:

IV

A ghost-girl-rider. And though, toil-tried,
    He withers daily,
    Time touches her not,
    But she still rides gaily
    In his rapt thought
    On that shagged and shaly
    Atlantic spot,
    And as when first eyed
Draws rein and sings to the swing of the tide.

1913

10 LOVERS 50 POEMS

WE SAT AT THE WINDOW

We sat at the window looking out,
And the rain came down like silken strings
That Swithin's day. Each gutter and spout
Babbled unchecked in the busy way
    Of witless things:
Nothing to read, nothing to see
Seemed in that room for her and me
    On Swithin's day.

We were irked by the scene, by our own selves; yes,
For I did not know, nor did she infer
How much there was to read and guess
By her in me, and to see and crown
    By me in her.
Wasted were two souls in their prime,
And great was the waste, that July time
    When the rain came down.

Bournemouth, 1875

21

ON STURMINSTER FOOT-BRIDGE

(*Onomatopœic*)

Reticulations creep upon the slack stream's face
When the wind skims irritably past,
The current clucks smartly into each hollow place
That years of flood have scrabbled in the pier's
                                    sodden base;
The floating-lily leaves rot fast.

On a roof stand the swallows ranged in wistful
                                    waiting rows,
Till they arrow off and drop like stones
Among the eyot-withies at whose foot the river
                                    flows:
And beneath the roof is she who in the dark
                                    world shows
As a lattice-gleam when midnight moans.

10 LOVERS 50 POEMS

22

A TWO-YEARS' IDYLL

    Yes; such it was;
  Just those two seasons unsought,
Sweeping like summertide wind on our ways;
    Moving, as straws,
  Hearts quick as ours in those days;
Going like wind, too, and rated as nought
    Save as the prelude to plays
    Soon to come – larger, life-fraught:
      Yes; such it was.

    "Nought" it was called,
  Even by ourselves – that which springs
Out of the years for all flesh, first or last,
    Commonplace, scrawled
  Dully on days that go past.
Yet, all the while, it upbore us like wings
    Even in hours overcast:
    Aye, though this best thing of things,
      "Nought" it was called!

10 LOVERS 50 POEMS

What seems it now?
Lost: such beginning was all;
Nothing came after: romance straight forsook
Quickly somehow
Life when we sped from our nook,
Primed for new scenes with designs smart and tall...
– A preface without any book,
A trumpet uplipped, but no call;
That seems it now.

23

OVERLOOKING THE RIVER STOUR

The swallows flew in the curves of an eight
    Above the river-gleam
    In the wet June's last beam:
Like little crossbows animate
The swallows flew in the curves of an eight
    Above the river-gleam.

Planing up shavings of crystal spray
    A moor-hen darted out
    From the bank thereabout,
And through the stream-shine ripped his way;
Planing up shavings of crystal spray
    A moor-hen darted out.

Closed were the kingcups; and the mead
    Dripped in monotonous green,
    Though the day's morning sheen
Had shown it golden and honeybee'd;
Closed were the kingcups; and the mead
    Dripped in monotonous green.

10 LOVERS 50 POEMS

And never I turned my head, alack,
    While these things met my gaze
    Through the pane's drop-drenched glaze,
To see the more behind my back. . . .
O never I turned, but let, alack,
    These less things hold my gaze!

24

THE MUSICAL BOX

     Lifelong to be
Seemed the fair colour of the time;
That there was standing shadowed near
A spirit who sang to the gentle chime
Of the self-struck notes, I did not hear,
     I did not see.

     Thus did it sing
To the mindless lyre that played indoors
As she came to listen for me without:
"O value what the nonce outpours –
This best of life – that shines about
     Your welcoming!"

     I had slowed along
After the torrid hours were done,
Though still the posts and walls and road
Flung back their sense of the hot-faced sun,
And had walked by Stourside Mill, where broad
     Stream-lilies throng.

10 LOVERS 50 POEMS

THE MUSICAL BOX

     And I descried
The dusky house that stood apart,
And her, white-muslined, waiting there
In the porch with high-expectant heart,
While still the thin mechanic air
     Went on inside.

     At whiles would flit
Swart bats, whose wings, be-webbed and tanned,
Whirred like the wheels of ancient clocks:
She laughed a hailing as she scanned
Me in the gloom, the tuneful box
     Intoning it.

     Lifelong to be
I thought it. That there watched hard by
A spirit who sang to the indoor tune,
"O make the most of what is nigh!"
I did not hear in my dull soul-swoon –
     I did not see.

10 LOVERS 50 POEMS

FLORENCE HENNIKER

10 LOVERS 50 POEMS

CHAPTER 6
FLORENCE HENNIKER

Hardy met Florence Henniker in 1893, at a time when the rift between him and Emma was widening. Florence was an author and journalist, married to an army officer. Hardy's (auto) biography says that "some of his best short poems were inspired by her."[xl]

Hardy describes his longing for a physical relationship with Florence, and her refusal, in "A Thunderstorm in Town". [xli] The first stanza builds up the intimacy of a moment together in the privacy of a hansom cab, the second uses a different rhyming scheme to emphasise the change, as the moment when he might have kissed her is lost and she leaps out at the first possible opportunity.

The same pattern unfolds when Hardy meets with Florence "At An Inn" in Winchester. The poem's short two-beat lines are initially used to emphasise the staff's perception of their intimacy: "...more than friends/...love's own pair." But towards the end of the poem their brevity is used to stress the blunt reality of unrequited love: "Love lingered numb."

"Wessex Heights" begins not with his hopes for a romance with Florence but with his gloomy feelings of exclusion from society (following the negative critical reaction to "Jude the Obscure").[xlii] Then a sudden rhyming of two short adjectives emphasises the depth of his sadness at her attitude to him: "As for one rare fair woman, I am now but a thought of hers,/I enter her mind and another thought succeeds me that she prefers."

"A Broken Appointment" continues this theme: "You did not come./You love not me," with perhaps a hint of petulance on Hardy's part. [xliii] But it ends on a moment of hope, with the repeated line "You love not me" now ending with a question-mark.

And it turned out that the relationship was to flourish, as a lasting platonic friendship. Florence became an important muse of Hardy's and the two of them co-authored the stories "The Spectre of the Real" in 1894 and "Contrasts" in 1903. They met from time to time and corresponded profusely. In 1911, Hardy wrote to her: "It occurred to me the other day that this year completes the eighteenth of our friendship. That is rather good as between man & woman, which is usually so brittle." [xliv]

This continued through into the period of Hardy's second marriage. In 1922, Hardy published "Without, Not Within Her", which appears to be about Florence Henniker. [xlv] One interpretation of this poem is that her influence had been able to drive out his demons, in particular his obsession with death: "It was that strange freshness you carried/into a soul/...And out from his spirit flew death".

The final meeting between Hardy and Florence Henniker was in midsummer 1922, when she came to stay at Max Gate. She died in April 1923.

FLORENCE HENNIKER

10 LOVERS 50 POEMS

25

A THUNDERSTORM IN TOWN
(A Reminiscence: 1893)

She wore a new "terra-cotta" dress,
And we stayed, because of the pelting storm,
Within the hansom's dry recess,
Though the horse had stopped; yea, motionless
    We sat on, snug and warm.

Then the downpour ceased, to my sharp sad pain,
And the glass that had screened our forms before
Flew up, and out she sprang to her door:
I should have kissed her if the rain
    Had lasted a minute more.

10 LOVERS 50 POEMS

26

AT AN INN

When we as strangers sought
    Their catering care,
Veiled smiles bespoke their thought
    Of what we were.
They warmed as they opined
    Us more than friends –
That we had all resigned
    For love's dear ends.

And that swift sympathy
    With living love
Which quicks the world – maybe
    The spheres above,
Made them our ministers,
    Moved them to say,
"Ah, God, that bliss like theirs
    Would flush our day!"

And we were left alone
    As Love's own pair;
Yet never the love-light shone
    Between us there!
But that which chilled the breath
    Of afternoon,
And palsied unto death
    The pane-fly's tune.

10 LOVERS 50 POEMS

AT AN INN

The kiss their zeal foretold,
    And now deemed come,
Came not: within his hold
    Love lingered numb.
Why cast he on our port
    A bloom not ours?
Why shaped us for his sport
    In after-hours?

As we seemed we were not
    That day afar,
And now we seem not what
    We aching are.
O severing sea and land,
    O laws of men,
Ere death, once let us stand
    As we stood then!

27

A BROKEN APPOINTMENT

      You did not come,
And marching Time drew on, and wore me numb. –
Yet less for loss of your dear presence there
Than that I thus found lacking in your make
That high compassion which can overbear
Reluctance for pure loving kindness' sake
Grieved I, when, as the hope-hour stroked its sum,
      You did not come.

      You love not me,
And love alone can lend you loyalty;
– I know and knew it. But, unto the store
Of human deeds divine in all but name,
Was it not worth a little hour or more
To add yet this: Once you, a woman, came
To soothe a time-torn man; even though it be
      You love not me?

10 LOVERS 50 POEMS

28

WESSEX HEIGHTS

There are some heights in Wessex, shaped as if by a kindly hand
For thinking, dreaming, dying on, and at crises when I stand,
Say, on Ingpen Beacon eastward, or on Wylls-Neck westwardly,
I seem where I was before my birth, and after death may be.

In the lowlands I have no comrade, not even the lone man's friend –
Her who suffereth long and is kind; accepts what he is too weak to mend:
Down there they are dubious and askance; there nobody thinks as I,
But mind-chains do not clank where one's next neighbour is the sky.

10 LOVERS 50 POEMS

In the towns I am tracked by phantoms having
>   weird detective ways –

Shadows of beings who fellowed with myself of
>   earlier days:

They hang about at places, and they say harsh heavy
>   things –

Men with a wintry sneer, and women with tart
>   disparagings.

Down there I seem to be false to myself, my simple
>   self that was,

And is not now, and I see him watching, wondering
>   what crass cause

Can have merged him into such a strange
>   continuator as this,

Who yet has something in common with himself,
>   my chrysalis.

I cannot go to the great grey Plain; there's a figure
>   against the moon,

Nobody sees it but I, and it makes my breast beat
>   out of tune;

I cannot go to the tall-spired town, being barred by
>   the forms now passed

For everybody but me, in whose long vision they
>   stand there fast.

10 LOVERS 50 POEMS

There's a ghost at Yell'ham Bottom chiding loud at
                            the fall of the night,
There's a ghost in Froom-side Vale, thin-lipped and
                            vague, in a shroud of white,
There is one in the railway train whenever I do not
                            want it near,
I see its profile against the pane, saying what I
                            would not hear.

As for one rare fair woman, I am now but a thought
                            of hers,
I enter her mind and another thought succeeds me
                            that she prefers;
Yet my love for her in its fulness she herself even
                            did not know;
Well, time cures hearts of tenderness, and now I can
                            let her go.

So I am found on Ingpen Beacon, or on Wylls-Neck
                            to the west,
Or else on homely Bulbarrow, or little Pilsdon
                            Crest,
Where men have never cared to haunt, nor women
                            have walked with me,
And ghosts then keep their distance; and I know
                            some liberty.

1896

10 LOVERS 50 POEMS

29

WITHOUT, NOT WITHIN HER

It was what you bore with you, Woman,
        Not inly were,
That throned you from all else human,
        However fair!

It was that strange freshness you carried
        Into a soul
Whereon no thought of yours tarried
        Two moments at all.

And out from his spirit flew death,
        And bale, and ban,
Like the corn-chaff under the breath
        Of the winnowing-fan.

EMMA - THE SADNESS COMES

10 LOVERS 50 POEMS

CHAPTER 7
EMMA - THE SADNESS COMES

By the mid 1890s, Hardy had become a major literary figure and he and Emma had been married for some two decades, but since leaving Sturminster, the gap between them had been widening. In 1883, just as he started work on Max Gate, the house near Dorchester that was to be their permanent home, Hardy had written "He Abjures Love", in which he seems to feel that he can never be capable of love again: "...after love what comes?/A scene that lours,/A few sad vacant hours." This unhappiness within the marriage continued into the next decade, setting the background for Hardy to start romancing Florence Henniker in 1893 (as described in the previous chapter).

After that relationship settled into a platonic friendship, Hardy and Emma enjoyed some happier times together for a while. She embraced the new bicycle craze, riding 50 miles a day [xlvi] and persuaded Hardy to get his own machine, the couple taking an eight week cycling holiday together in Summer 1896 in England and Belgium which he described as "an agreeable and instructive time".[xlvii]

But this seems to have been a short respite in a broader move towards a deeper rift. One cause was that Emma "had the fixed idea that she was the superior of her husband in birth, education, talents, and manners. She could not, and never did, recognise his greatness", according to Christine Wood-Homer, a regular visitor to the Hardy home.[xlviii] More potently, there is evidence that Emma suffered from mental illness, though at today's distance it is difficult to gauge how real this was. Eyewitness reports are sometimes coloured by personal animosity, and may simply describe characteristics such as an abrupt nature.

Hardy himself seems to have been in no doubt. His poem "The Interloper" is subtitled "And I saw the figure and visage of Madness seeking for a home".[l] It describes a sinister third presence that comes between an outwardly happy couple. In the final line of the first stanza Hardy says of this unwanted intruder "Whom I like not to be there!" and he emphasises this message by repeating it, using different words, at the end of all the other stanzas.

By using the imagery of an interloping presence "under which best lives corrode", Hardy separates Emma from the madness, making it easier for him to express continued love and respect for her even though she has outwardly changed.[li] He takes this even further in "At The Piano" where the madness now takes outright physical form: "A cowled Apparition/Came pushing between."

In 1899 Emma moved upstairs into her own separate set of rooms. Visitors to Max Gate can still climb the narrow steps that lead up to her cramped attic quarters. Emma called this "my sweet refuge and solace"[lii] and a year later one of her poems was published for the first time: "Spring Song" appearing in the popular journal *The Sphere*, followed by "The Gardener's Ruse" in *The Academy and Literature* in 1902.[liii]

Hardy does not seem to have shared Emma's positive view of these new arrangements. "The Ghost of the Past" describes "...a spectral housekeeping/... As daily I went up the stair/And down the stair." And in late 1901 he published "The Dame of Athelhall", its theme is a married couple who both love others. The husband believes: "A quick divorce; she will make him hers/And I wed mine", but the wife has just parted from her lover, believing that her duty lies within the marriage.

Hardy wrote to Athelhampton's owner: "I send on with much pleasure the copy of the poems I had reserved for you. You will find the story of the irresolute lady who lived in your house at p. 182. I don't want to alarm you, but I fancy that the brief remainder of her life was unhappy, & that she 'walks' in the Hall, occasionally." Hardy and Emma had visited Athelhampton for dinner on a number of occasions and he may be imagining her there as the "unhappy" lady from whom he wants a divorce, though the process in Victorian England was not easy.

In 1905, Hardy met Florence Dugdale and started a relationship that was to intensify over subsequent years and ultimately lead to marriage after Emma's death (this and other matters relating to Florence are described in greater detail in the next chapter). While Hardy took Florence with him to stay with his friends, Emma became more involved in her campaigning activities, both on animal rights and on women's suffrage. Not only did she attend the large

London marches in favour of votes for women in 1907 and 1908, she also published articles on political reform, most notably in *The Nation*, a leading radical weekly and forerunner of today's *New Statesman* whose eminent contributors at the time included Bertrand Russell. In a strange development, Emma in 1910 became friends with Florence, who helped submit her fictional work to publishers and produce self-published versions. But Emma was sickening and taking opium, a widely-used painkiller at the time, and in November 1912 she passed away.

The final group of poems chosen for this section are from the much-praised group of 1912-13 eulogies written just after Emma's death. "The Voice" seems to refer back to the madness that had altered her, hoping it is no longer there after death, and that the old Emma has been restored: "...call to me,/Saying that now you are not as you were/When you had changed..." For a moment in the second stanza, these thoughts become stronger and visual, as Hardy envisages Emma in her "...air-blue gown"; but then the vision fades away. "A Dream or No" refers to the same theme of how she had changed, thinking sadly back to the happy days at St Juliot and lamenting: "But nought of that maid from Saint-Juliot I see."

"The Walk" picks up the simple yet deep sadness of bereavement: "You did not walk with me/Of late to the hill-top tree", adding, "As in earlier days;/You were weak and lame." There is a different emphasis in "Without Ceremony", which speaks almost resentfully about Emma's death, comparing it to the way that in life she would suddenly disappear: "it was your way, my dear,/To be gone without a word."

After Emma passed away, her niece Lilian and Hardy's sister Kate moved in to Max Gate. While they organised the housekeeping, he struggled with legal arrangements and correspondence. The poem "A Circular" describes the pangs of bereavement through the pain he experienced when doing this. The initial tone is almost jolly, with its description of the fine clothes on offer in the junk mail that continues to arrive for Emma. Then there is a powerful volta (change of tone) in the final line, where he describes how just the year before, she had been "costumed in a shroud."

To provide further support at this terrible time, Hardy wrote to ask Florence Dugdale to come and stay. Fifteen months later, they were to marry.

10 LOVERS 50 POEMS

HE ABJURES LOVE

At last I put off love,
    For twice ten years
The daysman of my thought,
    And hope, and doing;
Being ashamed thereof,
    And faint of fears
And desolations, wrought
    In his pursuing,

Since first in youthtime those
    Disquietings
That heart-enslavement brings
    To hale and hoary,
Became my housefellows,
    And, fool and blind,
I turned from kith and kind
    To give him glory.

10 LOVERS 50 POEMS

HE ABJURES LOVE

I was as children be
    Who have no care;
I did not shrink or sigh,
    I did not sicken;
But lo, Love beckoned me,
    And I was bare,
And poor, and starved, and dry,
    And fever-stricken.

Too many times ablaze
    With fatuous fires,
Enkindled by his wiles
    To new embraces,
Did I, by wilful ways
    And baseless ires,
Return the anxious smiles
    Of friendly faces.

HE ABJURES LOVE

No more will now rate I
    The common rare,
The midnight drizzle dew,
    The grey hour golden,
The wind a yearning cry,
    The faulty fair,
Things dreamt, of comelier hue
    Than things beholden! . . .

– I speak as one who plumbs
    Life's dim profound,
One who at length can sound
    Clear views and certain.
But – after love what comes?
    A scene that lours,
A few sad vacant hours,
    And then, the Curtain.

1883

10 LOVERS 50 POEMS

30

THE INTERLOPER

*"And I saw the figure and visage of Madness
seeking for a home"*

There are three folk driving in a quaint old chaise,
And the cliff-side track looks green and fair;
I view them talking in quiet glee
As they drop down towards the puffins' lair
    By the roughest of ways;
But another with the three rides on, I see,
    Whom I like not to be there!

No: it's not anybody you think of. Next
A dwelling appears by a slow sweet stream
Where two sit happy and half in the dark:
They read, helped out by a frail-wick'd gleam,
    Some rhythmic text;
But one sits with them whom they don't mark,
    One I'm wishing could not be there.

10 LOVERS 50 POEMS

THE INTERLOPER

No: not whom you knew and name. And now
I discern gay diners in a mansion-place,
And the guests dropping wit – pert, prim, or choice,
And the hostess's tender and laughing face,
    And the host's bland brow;
But I cannot help hearing a hollow voice,
    And I'd fain not hear it there.

No: it's not from the stranger you met once. Ah,
Yet a goodlier scene than that succeeds;
People on a lawn – quite a crowd of them. Yes,
And they chatter and ramble as fancy leads;
    And they say, "Hurrah!"
To a blithe speech made; save one, mirthless,
    Who ought not to be there.

Nay: it's not the pale Form your imagings raise,
That waits on us all at a destined time,
It is not the Fourth Figure the Furnace showed;
O that it were such a shape sublime
    In these latter days!
It is that under which best lives corrode;
  Would, would it could not be there!

10 LOVERS 50 POEMS

31

AT THE PIANO

A woman was playing,
    A man looking on;
    And the mould of her face,
    And her neck, and her hair,
    Which the rays fell upon
    Of the two candles there,
Sent him mentally straying
    In some fancy-place
    Where pain had no trace.

A cowled Apparition
    Came pushing between;
    And her notes seemed to sigh;
    And the lights to burn pale,
    As a spell numbed the scene.
    But the maid saw no bale,
And the man no monition;
    And Time laughed awry,
    And the Phantom hid nigh.

32

THE GHOST OF THE PAST

We two kept house, the Past and I,
    The Past and I;
Through all my tasks it hovered nigh,
    Leaving me never alone.
It was a spectral housekeeping
    Where fell no jarring tone,
As strange, as still a housekeeping
    As ever has been known.

As daily I went up the stair
    And down the stair,
I did not mind the Bygone there –
    The Present once to me;
Its moving meek companionship
    I wished might ever be,
There was in that companionship
    Something of ecstasy.

10 LOVERS 50 POEMS

THE GHOST OF THE PAST

It dwelt with me just as it was,
    Just as it was
When first its prospects gave me pause
    In wayward wanderings,
Before the years had torn old troths
    As they tear all sweet things,
Before gaunt griefs had torn old troths
    And dulled old rapturings.

And then its form began to fade,
    Began to fade,
Its gentle echoes faintlier played
    At eves upon my ear
Than when the autumn's look embrowned
    The lonely chambers here,
When autumn's settling shades embrowned
    Nooks that it haunted near.

10 LOVERS 50 POEMS

THE GHOST OF THE PAST

And so with time my vision less,
    Yea, less and less
Makes of that Past my housemistress,
    It dwindles in my eye;
It looms a far-off skeleton
    And not a comrade nigh,
A fitful far-off skeleton
    Dimming as days draw by.

33

THE DAME OF ATHELHALL

I

"Dear! Shall I see thy face," she said,
    "In one brief hour!
And away with thee from a loveless bed
To a far-off sun, to a vine-wrapt bower,
And be thine own unseparated,
    And challenge the world's white glower?"

II

She quickened her feet, and met him where
    They had predesigned:
And they clasped, and mounted, and cleft the air
Upon whirling wheels; till the will to bind
Her life with his made the moments there
    Efface the years behind.

10 LOVERS 50 POEMS

III

Miles slid, and the port uprose to view
    As they sped on;
When slipping its bond the bracelet flew
From her fondled arm. Replaced anon,
Its cameo of the abjured one drew
    Her musings thereupon.

IV

The gaud with his image once had been
    A gift from him:
And so it was that its carving keen
Refurbished memories wearing dim,
Which set in her soul a twinge of teen,
    And a tear on her lashes' brim.

V

'I may not go!' she at length outspake,
    'Thoughts call me back –
I would still lose all for your dear, true sake;
My heart is thine, friend! But my track
Home, home to Athelhall I must take
    To hinder household wrack!'

10 LOVERS 50 POEMS

VI

He was wroth. And they parted, weak and wan;
    And he left the shore;
His ship diminished, was low, was gone;
And she heard in the waves as the daytide wore,
And read in the leer of the sun that shone,
    That they parted for evermore.

VII

She homed as she came, at the dip of eve
    On Athel Coomb
Regaining the Hall she had sworn to leave.
The house was soundless as a tomb,
And she stole to her chamber, there to grieve
    Lone, kneeling, in the gloom.

VIII

From the lawn without rose her husband's voice
    To one his friend:
'Another her Love, another my choice,
Her going is good. Our conditions mend;
In a change of mates we shall both rejoice;
    I hoped that it thus might end!

10 LOVERS 50 POEMS

IX

'A quick divorce; she will make him hers,
    And I wed mine.
So Time rights all things in long, long years –
Or rather she, by her bold design!
I admire a woman no balk deters:
    She has blessed my life, in fine.

X

'I shall build new rooms for my new true bride,
    Let the bygone be:
By now, no doubt, she has crossed the tide
With the man to her mind. Far happier she
In some warm vineland by his side
 Than ever she was with me.'

36

THE VOICE

Woman much missed, how you call to me, call to me,
Saying that now you are not as you were
When you had changed from the one who was
                                  all to me,
But as at first, when our day was fair.

Can it be you that I hear? Let me view you, then,
Standing as when I drew near to the town
Where you would wait for me: yes, as I knew
                                  you then,
Even to the original air-blue gown!

Or is it only the breeze, in its listlessness
Travelling across the wet mead to me here,
You being ever dissolved to wan wistlessness,
Heard no more again far or near?

Thus I; faltering forward,
Leaves around me falling,
Wind oozing thin through the thorn from norward
And the woman calling.

December 1912

10 LOVERS 50 POEMS

A DREAM OR NO

Why go to Saint-Juliot? What's Juliot to me?
Some strange necromancy
But charmed me to fancy
That much of my life claims the spot as its key.

Yes. I have had dreams of that place in the West,
And a maiden abiding
Thereat as in hiding;
Fair-eyed and white-shouldered, broad-browed
                                 and brown-tressed.

And of how, coastward bound on a night long ago,
There lonely I found her,
The sea-birds around her,
And other than nigh things uncaring to know.

So sweet her life there (in my thought has it seemed)
That quickly she drew me
To take her unto me,
And lodge her long years with me. Such have I
                                 dreamed.

10 LOVERS 50 POEMS

But nought of that maid from Saint-Juliot I see;
Can she ever have been here,
And shed her life's sheen here,
The woman I thought a long housemate with me?

Does there even a place like Saint-Juliot exist?
Or a Vallency Valley
With stream and leafed alley,
Or Beeny, or Bos with its flounce flinging mist?

February 1913

10 LOVERS 50 POEMS

39

THE WALK

You did not walk with me
Of late to the hill-top tree
    By the gated ways,
    As in earlier days;
    You were weak and lame,
    So you never came,
And I went alone, and I did not mind,
Not thinking of you as left behind.

I walked up there to-day
Just in the former way;
    Surveyed around
    The familiar ground
    By myself again:
    What difference, then?
Only that underlying sense
Of the look of a room on returning thence.

37

WITHOUT CEREMONY

It was your way, my dear,
To vanish without a word
When callers, friends, or kin
Had left, and I hastened in
To rejoin you, as I inferred.

And when you'd a mind to career
Off anywhere – say to town –
You were all on a sudden gone
Before I had thought thereon,
Or noticed your trunks were down.

So, now that you disappear
For ever in that swift style,
Your meaning seems to me
Just as it used to be:
"Good-bye is not worth while!"

38

A CIRCULAR

As "legal representative"
I read a missive not my own,
On new designs the senders give
    For clothes, in tints as shown.

Here figure blouses, gowns for tea,
And presentation-trains of state,
Charming ball-dresses, millinery,
    Warranted up to date.

And this gay-pictured, spring-time shout
Of Fashion, hails what lady proud?
Her who before last year ebbed out
    Was costumed in a shroud.

10 LOVERS 50 POEMS

FLORENCE DUGDALE

10 LOVERS 50 POEMS

CHAPTER 8
FLORENCE DUGDALE

Florence Dugdale (1879-1937) started her professional life as a schoolteacher and journalist, and in 1905 was building her career as a writer. That year, she was introduced to Hardy by the poet A H Hyatt. She sent Hardy flowers and he reciprocated with a copy of his *Wessex Poems*.[lvi] She visited him that August at Max Gate, while Emma worked up in her attic room, and before long he commissioned her to research material for the third part of his epic 600-page poem *The Dynasts*.[lvii]

The early passion that Hardy felt for Florence is powerfully expressed in "After the Visit", written within months of their first meeting.[lviii] The marvellous alliteration "large luminous living eyes" draws the reader in to Hardy's romantic feelings.[lix]

There is a sober ending to this poem: "That which mattered most could not be", implying that Hardy felt the relationship could not develop. However, this was wrong; it turned out to develop a long way, even over the next few years while Emma was still alive.

By early 1907, Hardy and Florence were meeting together[lx] in London at a time when Emma was not in town and that April, after a research session together at the British Museum, he describes their temporary parting at a railway station in "On the

Departure Platform".[lxi] The poem begins with a kiss – a sharp contrast with the failed intimacy with Florence Henniker – and as Hardy watches his lover disappearing into the crowd in her white muslin dress he describes her as: "...she who was more than my life to me."

In August 1909 Hardy's letters record him staying for ten days with his "young friend and assistant" as a house guest of his friend Edward Clodd in Aldeburgh; Emma was not present. A couple of months later, the couple made a "surreptitious trip" to Chichester and a few months later they were in the Isle of Wight together. In parallel with these trysts, Hardy helped Florence contact publishers and they collaborated on literary projects.[lxiii]

In mid-1910, a new development in this love triangle saw Florence introduce herself to Emma at the women-only Lyceum Club[lxiv] in London. Their acquaintance flourished. Florence spent many weeks at Max Gate in the second half of the year at Emma's invitation, helping her by typing up her novella *The Maid on the Shore*, written when Hardy had been courting her four decades earlier, and supporting her networking with publishers. In a sign of how important this new friendship had become to Emma, she angrily refused to let Hardy take Florence to visit his siblings that Christmas due to her concern that they would deliberately damage it. The friendship then continued, though the two women now tended to meet away from Max Gate, thus avoiding Hardy. In parallel, Florence and Hardy spent time with one another but without Emma, notably repeating their trip to the Clodd home several times.[lxv]

FLORENCE DUGDALE

Florence moved into Max Gate some months after Emma's death in late 1912 and in February 1914 she married Hardy, having endured a year in which he had poured out his grief at Emma's death in the "Poems of 1912-13" (see the previous chapter). After the wedding, Hardy's misery over his private loss ebbed, only to be replaced months later by a broader angst as Britain entered the First World War: "On this day at Athelhampton... a telegram came announcing the fact. ... The whole news... burst upon Hardy's mind next morning ... he felt it would be... untold disaster."[lxvi]

Hardy turned 80 in 1920, two years after the war's end, and was still enjoying an active life with Florence.[lxvii] "A Jog-Trot Pair", published in 1922, is a paean to the quiet joys of marriage, the pleasures that lie beyond passion. The rhythm of the words feels like a gentle jogging horse-ride "hither and back", echoed by the pattern of the lines: two long ones extending far to the right followed by a short one. The poem's message is reinforced by the repeated emphasis on the delights of "simple things".

Another poem about Florence also appeared in 1922. Hardy dedicated "I Sometimes Think" to her and it speaks of her love for him in a world that misunderstands him: "For one did care,/...Cares still, heeds all, and will, even though/I may despair."

However, it feels more self-centred and lacks the sheer joy of a couple together he had shown in "A Jog-Trot Pair", perhaps reflecting the focus on his own needs – demonstrated by the incident one night when "someone at Athelhampton Hall had been taking [Florence] to Christian Science meetings and one evening she was late returning...he became annoyed as it was after his dinner hour."[lxviii]

In 1924 Florence was diagnosed with cancer. She went to London for an operation and Hardy, now finding travel difficult, arranged for his brother to bring her home in a hired car. "Nobody Comes" is dated to that very day, so we know it describes Hardy's anxiety as he waits deep into the night for them to return: "And mute by the gate I stand again alone/And nobody pulls up there."[lxix]

This can be read as a love poem by a husband concerned for his ailing wife, or as the inward-looking concerns of an old man for himself. There is a similar ambiguity in a story told by the maid Miss E. E. T. of Hardy coming to the kitchen that day to order lamb and suet jam as a special treat for Florence – who on returning was apparently upset because this was not in fact what she liked.[lxx]

However, during Hardy's last illness just before he died in 1928, Florence "hardly left her husband's side."[lxxi] Some insights into her feelings are given by letters she wrote to Harold Barlow, a former pupil, who had emigrated to Africa. She had written to him when she married Hardy to say that it was a "genuine love match" to "one of the kindest, most humane men in the world" and then in 1932 she wrote: "I am writing this late in the evening alone, in the room where I first met my husband...I thank you for your kind words of sympathy about my great loss. It was such a wonderful thing to live in close association with that great mind & that noble personality. After having lived fourteen years with such a companion it is little wonder that I feel intolerably lonely – & find the world very empty."[lxxii]

Florence herself lived into her late 50s and passed away in 1937.

34

AFTER THE VISIT

(To F.E.D.)

    Come again to the place
Where your presence was as a leaf that skims
Down a drouthy way whose ascent bedims
        The bloom on the farer's face.

    Come again, with the feet
That were light on the green as a thistledown ball,
And those mute ministrations to one and to all
        Beyond a man's saying sweet.

    Until then the faint scent
Of the bordering flowers swam unheeded away,
And I marked not the charm in the changes of day
        As the cloud-colours came and went.

    Through the dark corridors
Your walk was so soundless I did not know
Your form from a phantom's of long ago
        Said to pass on the ancient floors,

10 LOVERS 50 POEMS

    Till you drew from the shade,
And I saw the large luminous living eyes
Regard me in fixed inquiring-wise
        As those of a soul that weighed,

        Scarce consciously,
The eternal question of what Life was,
And why we were there, and by whose strange laws
        That which mattered most could not be.

10 LOVERS 50 POEMS

35

ON THE DEPARTURE PLATFORM

We kissed at the barrier; and passing through
She left me, and moment by moment got
Smaller and smaller, until to my view
    She was but a spot;

A wee white spot of muslin fluff
That down the diminishing platform bore
Through hustling crowds of gentle and rough
    To the carriage door.

Under the lamplight's fitful glowers,
Behind dark groups from far and near,
Whose interests were apart from ours,
    She would disappear,

Then show again, till I ceased to see
That flexible form, that nebulous white;
And she who was more than my life to me
    Had vanished quite. . . .

10 LOVERS 50 POEMS

We have penned new plans since that fair fond day,
And in season she will appear again –
Perhaps in the same soft white array –
    But never as then!

– "And why, young man, must eternally fly
A joy you'll repeat, if you love her well?"
– O friend, nought happens twice thus; why,
    I cannot tell!

10 LOVERS 50 POEMS

40

A JOG-TROT PAIR

Who were the twain that trod this track
So many times together
Hither and back,
In spells of certain and uncertain weather?

Commonplace in conduct they
Who wandered to and fro here
Day by day:
Two that few dwellers troubled themselves
                                    to know here.

The very gravel-path was prim
That daily they would follow:
Borders trim:
Never a wayward sprout, or hump, or hollow.

Trite usages in tamest style
Had tended to their plighting.
"It's just worth while,
Perhaps," they had said. "And saves much sad
                                    good-nighting."

10 LOVERS 50 POEMS

And petty seemed the happenings
        That ministered to their joyance:
      Simple things,
Onerous to satiate souls, increased their buoyance.

Who could those common people be,
        Of days the plainest, barest?
      They were we;
Yes; happier than the cleverest, smartest, rarest.

41

I SOMETIMES THINK

(*For F.E.H.*)

I sometimes think as here I sit
      Of things I have done,
Which seemed in doing not unfit
      To face the sun:
Yet never a soul has paused a whit
      On such – not one.

There was that eager strenuous press
      To sow good seed;
There was that saving from distress
      In the nick of need;
There were those words in the wilderness:
      Who cared to heed?

Yet can this be full true, or no?
      For one did care,
And, spiriting into my house, to, fro,
      Like wind on the stair,
Cares still, heeds all, and will, even though
      I may despair.

10 LOVERS 50 POEMS

42

NOBODY COMES

Tree-leaves labour up and down,
      And through them the fainting light
      Succumbs to the crawl of night.
Outside in the road the telegraph wire
      To the town from the darkening land
Intones to travellers like a spectral lyre
      Swept by a spectral hand.

A car comes up, with lamps full-glare,
      That flash upon a tree:
      It has nothing to do with me,
And whangs along in a world of its own,
      Leaving a blacker air;
And mute by the gate I stand again alone,
      And nobody pulls up there.

9 October 1924

10 LOVERS 50 POEMS

GERTRUDE BUGLER

10 LOVERS 50 POEMS

CHAPTER 9
GERTRUDE BUGLER

In 1913, still in mourning for Emma, Hardy met Gertrude Bugler who at age 16 was one of the amateur acting troupe The Hardy Players who were performing dramatisations of his work. He saw her at subsequent performances in 1916 and 1920 and became greatly impressed with her acting skills, though Florence did not agree. He also learned that her mother was the milkmaid, a brief sight of whom decades earlier had given him inspiration for Tess in his great novel by that name.

After the 1920 performances, Florence wrote: "T H has lost his heart to [Gertrude] entirely, but as she is soon getting married I don't let that cast me down too much."[lxxiii] Gertrude moved away from Dorchester deep into the Dorset countryside to live with her husband. By 1924 she had a small baby, and she assumed that her acting days were over. But The Hardy Players were planning a production of *Tess*, and Hardy was determined that Gertrude would play the leading role. Arrangements were made for childcare and Gertrude took the slow and circuitous route by bus and train to Dorchester to attend rehearsals. The resulting performances were highly successful, applauded not only by Hardy but also by a review in *The Times*, with particular praise for Gertrude.

Hardy had invited the great actress Sybil Thorndike to watch these shows, and through her contacts, a serious offer was made for Gertrude to transfer to London to perform her role as Tess in the West End. This was accepted and again, childcare arrangements were prepared.

But Florence had become increasingly agitated, her letters revealing both jealousy and concern that others might perceive an improper relationship between Hardy and Gertrude. She sent a telegram to Gertrude inviting herself to the house in the countryside, and when she arrived she insisted that the young actress must withdraw from the London performances, which is what happened.[lxxiv]

Hardy wrote the poem "An Expostulation" about these events. Its theme is that Gertrude is so precious to the local community ("We...count few Wessex daughters half so dear") that she has no need to face the pitfalls of London life. There is no call for the trappings of the big city, symbolised by the application of make-up, when she naturally has such "bloomfullness".

Yet, it was Hardy himself who had been the force behind arranging for Gertrude to go to London, and Florence who had stopped that happening. So, this poem reads as a strange justification after the event for why she should not go, that is not reflective of Hardy's true feelings.

The last time that Hardy met Gertrude was when the initial arrangements for her transfer to London were being made. After the trip was abandoned, the two never saw one another again, with Hardy passing away in 1928.

After his death, Florence, perhaps feeling guilty at what she had done, helped in reviving the plan and Gertrude did finally appear successfully on the West End stage. She lived a long life and a fascinating video interview with her is available describing these events.[lxxv]

43

AN EXPOSTULATION

Why want to go afar
      Where pitfalls are,
When all we swains adore
Your featness more and more
As heroine of our artless masquings here,
And count few Wessex' daughters half so dear?

Why paint your appealing face,
      When its born grace
Is such no skill can match
With powder, puff, or patch,
Whose every touch defames your bloomfulness,
And with each stain increases our distress?

Yea, is it not enough
      That (rare or rough
Your lines here) all uphold you,
And as with wings enfold you,
But you must needs desert the kine-cropt vale
  Wherein your foredames gaily filled the pail?

10 LOVERS 50 POEMS

CHAPTER 10
END-POEM

When Hardy wrote "The Children and Sir Nameless" at age 82, he still had several years of poetry-writing ahead of him, but it is chosen as the last poem in this collection for it touches on many themes about a life drawing towards its end.

Perhaps Hardy is reminding himself that his fame, like the power of Ozymandias in Shelley's poem, would not last forever; maybe he is warning himself not to be angry towards children. He is probably having a dig at the Victorian church-restorers who he and other members of the Society for Protection of Ancient Buildings felt had ruined Puddletown Church – despite a heated campaign to save it – and he has taken another opportunity to mention Athelhampton, whose builders, the Martyn family, are all buried in that church.

Although this touches on death, as so many of Hardy's poems do, there is an almost music-hall rhythm and gaiety to this poem. Perhaps Hardy was well aware that some people saw him as a grumpy old man, and he wanted to mock himself gently for having that reputation...

10 LOVERS 50 POEMS

44

THE CHILDREN
AND SIR NAMELESS

Sir Nameless, once of Athelhall, declared:
'These wretched children romping in my park
Trample the herbage till the soil is bared,
And yap and yell from early morn till dark!
Go keep them harnessed to their set routines:
Thank God I've none to hasten my decay;
For green remembrance there are better means
Than offspring, who but wish their sires away.'

Sir Nameless of that mansion said anon:
'To be perpetuate for my mightiness
Sculpture must image me when I am gone.'
– He forthwith summoned carvers there express
To shape a figure stretching seven-odd feet
(For he was tall) in alabaster stone,
With shield, and crest, and casque, and sword
                                        complete:
When done a statelier work was never known.

10 LOVERS 50 POEMS

Three hundred years hied; Church-restorers came,
And, no one of his lineage being traced,
They thought an effigy so large in frame
Best fitted for the floor. There it was placed,
Under the seats for schoolchildren. And they
Kicked out his name, and hobnailed off his nose;
And, as they yawn through sermon-time, they say,
'Who was this old stone man beneath our toes?'

10 LOVERS 50 POEMS

CHAPTER 11
MAKING FILMS

In 1911, Thomas Hardy signed his first contract for the filming of one of his works, with a British company planning to make a movie based on Tess; a deal for two others followed soon after. Although none of these came to fruition, in 1913 a US company successfully brought another version of Tess to the big screen.

As we look back at this time, covering the final two years of his strained marriage to Emma and then the extraordinary emotion he penned in his elegies for her while Florence waited to marry him, it may seem incongruous to think of him checking screenplays and agreeing film royalties, like a modern author. Even more, he attended the glittering film premier at Pyke's Cinematograph Theatre in London's West End on 21st October 1913. Coming less than a year after Emma's death, perhaps this helps us understand a little more the complex emotions he felt at this time.

Hardy initially expressed uncertainty about the new medium, noting that "I was interested in it as a scientific toy," but at the same time he was becoming convinced of the merits of dramatising his work for the stage. He wrote the script for the stage adaptation of Tess and, although still in mourning, took a keen interest in its production in Dorchester. This was where he first saw Gertrude Bugler. After this, his early doubts about film seem to have lessened and he engaged with both cinematic and stage adaptations of his novels throughout most of the remainder of his life.

He scrutinised numerous film scripts, rejecting many as poor representations of his work, and accepting just three more: Far From the Madding Crowd in 1916, The Mayor of Casterbridge in 1921 and a remake of Tess by Metro Goldwyn Mayer in 1924, which paid $50,000 for the rights. The Mayor was shot in Dorset by a small British company based in Shoreham by Sea and Hardy visited the set, commenting *they asked us to come as see the process. The result is that I have been talking to the Mayor, Mrs Henchard, Eliz. Jane, & the rest, in the flesh...* In parallel, he was closely involved in scripting and viewing further stage productions, culminating in Gertrude Bugler's performance as Tess in Dorchester and Florence's veto of her acting in London, as described in Chapter 9 above.

After Hardy's death, his novels have continued as a popular subject for filmmakers across the decades, right up to the 2020s, with repeated remakes of, in particular, Tess and Far From the Madding Crowd.

By comparison, filming of his poems has been minimal compared to his output of almost 1000 poems. There are a smattering of readings, of which a few are dramatised, on YouTube and similar streaming services.

The 10 Lovers, 50 Poems project of some fifty short videos, each focussed on just one of the poems in this book, thus broaches new ground as a large-scale filming of Hardy's verses. Yet it also builds on a filmic tradition stretching right back to Hardy's lifetime, particularly the 1921 Mayor, since all the videos have been filmed in Dorset and, like that work by the Progress Film Company, they are made by a production team based locally and drawing on local acting talent. And, just as Hardy initially released his earlier novels as serials, so the 10 Lovers, 50 Poems films are initially released at two-week intervals.

Most of the filming took place at Athelhampton in the heart of Dorset, with its close connections to Hardy from his grandfather's birth through to his regular visits into his final years, as described in earlier chapters. The actors and readers are mainly from the New Hardy Players, the local group that continues the tradition of those who worked with Hardy himself, and from the Dorchester Youth Theatre. Some have since the filming started courses at RADA in London as they develop their acting careers. The Directors, Howard Payton and Alison Payton, have long and distinguished careers in film and theatre and have worked on this project with an experienced camera and sound team. Concept and executive production is by the writer of this book; a full list of everyone involved and their roles in given in the list.

Each individual video is comprised of three parts. Initially, there is a "semi-dramatised" reading of the poem, with the words spoken while actors play out the events and emotions Hardy describes. In the second part, there are pertinent interviews with modern poets, with experts from the Hardy Society, with local people whose relatives knew Hardy or who know the area well, and with authors of novels and biographies about him. These interviews explain who each poem is believed to refer to, the stage of Hardy's life and the emotions he expresses, while also critically examining its relevance to modern life — and describing the poetical techniques he uses. Finally, there is another reading of the poem, but this time the words scroll slowly across the screen, allowing the viewer to connect the spoken and written words — and to perhaps understand the poem in a different way from the beginning, now being informed by themes drawn out in the discussion.

While each video is complete in itself, taken together they build up the entire story of Thomas Hardy's romantic life, from those earliest teenage loves right through to his time with Gertrude Bugler in his 80s. So, just as with this book, it is possible to enjoy each video and poem individually, as well as taking them together as a whole to understand how Hardy's love life and emotions developed — in his own words.

FILM PRODUCTION TEAM

Executive Producer & Writer
Giles Keating

Producer, Director & Photographer
Howard Payton

Assistant Director & Production Manager
Alison Payton

Camera
Ian Condon

Sound Recordist
Andy Worth

Editing
Ian Condon
Howard Payton

Costumes & Props
Alison Payton
Lou Pugh

Music
Tim Laycock

Musicians
Angela Laycock
Tim Laycock
Fiona Staddon
Mike Staddon
Lucy Sturge

Presenters
Giles Keating
Owen Davies
Alison Payton

LEAD ACTORS

Thomas Hardy
Jonathan White
Samuel Kelly
Chris Pullen

Emma Hardy
Amelia Chorley
Alison Payton
Lou Pugh

Florence Hardy
Liz Bennett

THE LOVERS

Lizbie Brown
Molly Flute

Retty
Bronwyn Fletcher

Eliza Nicholls & Mary Jane Nicholls
Eva Staddon

Mary Frances Scott Siddons
Tilda Sansom

Tryphena Sparks
Kate Braidwood

Florence Henniker
Dee Thorne

Gertrude Bugler
Susie King

ACTORS

Thomas Hardy's Father
Rod Whitemore

Jemima Hardy
Lucy Sturge

Vicar
Rod Drew

Country Girl
Eva Staddon

Melia
Hannah Carolan

Celia
Lily Barrett

Tryphena's Child
Maddy Chapman

Waitress
Kelly Sage

Gentleman
Robin Mills

Cowled Figure
Devina Symes

Station Master
Hugh Chapman

Station Porter
Peter Allison

Sir Nameless
Alistair Chisholm

SUPPORTING ARTISTS

*Hilary Charlesworth, Mike Lofthouse,
Sue Lofthouse, Fran Sansom, Rob Sansom,
Maisie Sansom, Rebecca Dunn, Hugh Chapman,
Patsy Chapman, Heather Chapman,
Maddy Chapman, Sue Worth, Robin Mills,
Brian Caddy, Olive Sturge, Alban O'Brien,
Joy Parsons, Dave Parsons, Maya Pieris,
Helen Simpson, Sarah Stewart, Jim Stewart,
Barry White, Chrissie White, Mona Elkotory,
Zeph Staddon, Noah Hopkins,
Rufus Williams, Andy Hills, Linda Bolton,
Ella Trevorrow, Elli Viney, Bess Viney, Rosie Viney*

INTERVIEWEES

*Mark Damon Chutter, Thomas Hardy Society
Paula Byrne, Author "Hardy Women"
Elizabeth Lowry, Author "The Chosen"
Christopher Nicholson, Author "Winter"
Mariah Whelan, Poet "The Love I Do To You"
Rebecca Shipp, Thomas Hardy Society
Laura Mason*

WITH THANKS TO

*The New Hardy Players
Jo Simons, Dorchester Youth Theatre
A special thanks to Devina Symes for lending us
Gertrude Bugler's original cloak given to her by
Gertrude's sister Norrie Woodall.*

Amelia Chorley as Emma Gifford

Liz Bennett as Florence Dugdale

Molly Flute as Lizbie Brown

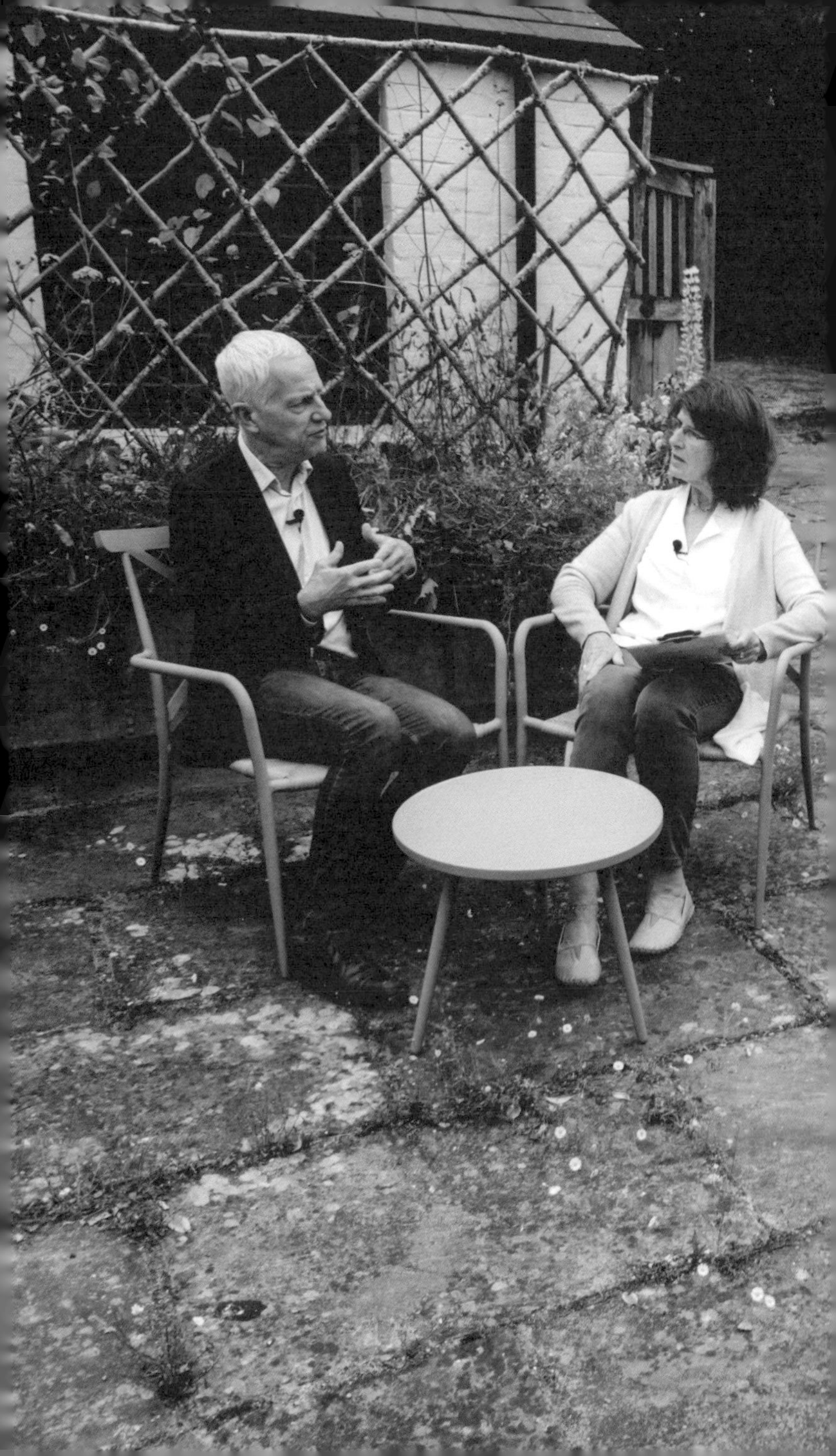

Giles Keating and Alison Payton with Ian Condon at the camera

Kate Braidwood as Tryphena Sparks

Tilda Sansom as Mary Frances Scott-Siddons

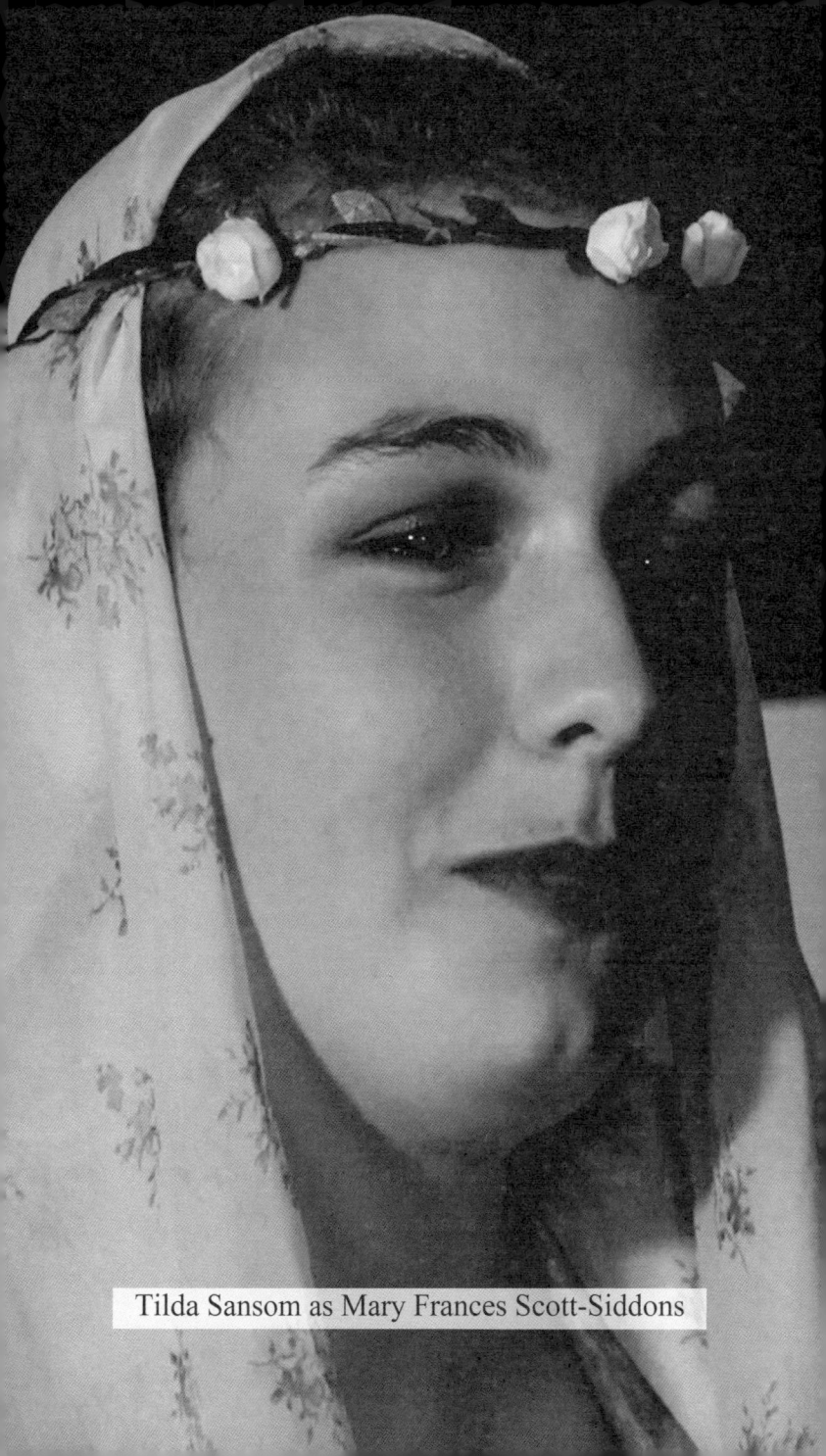

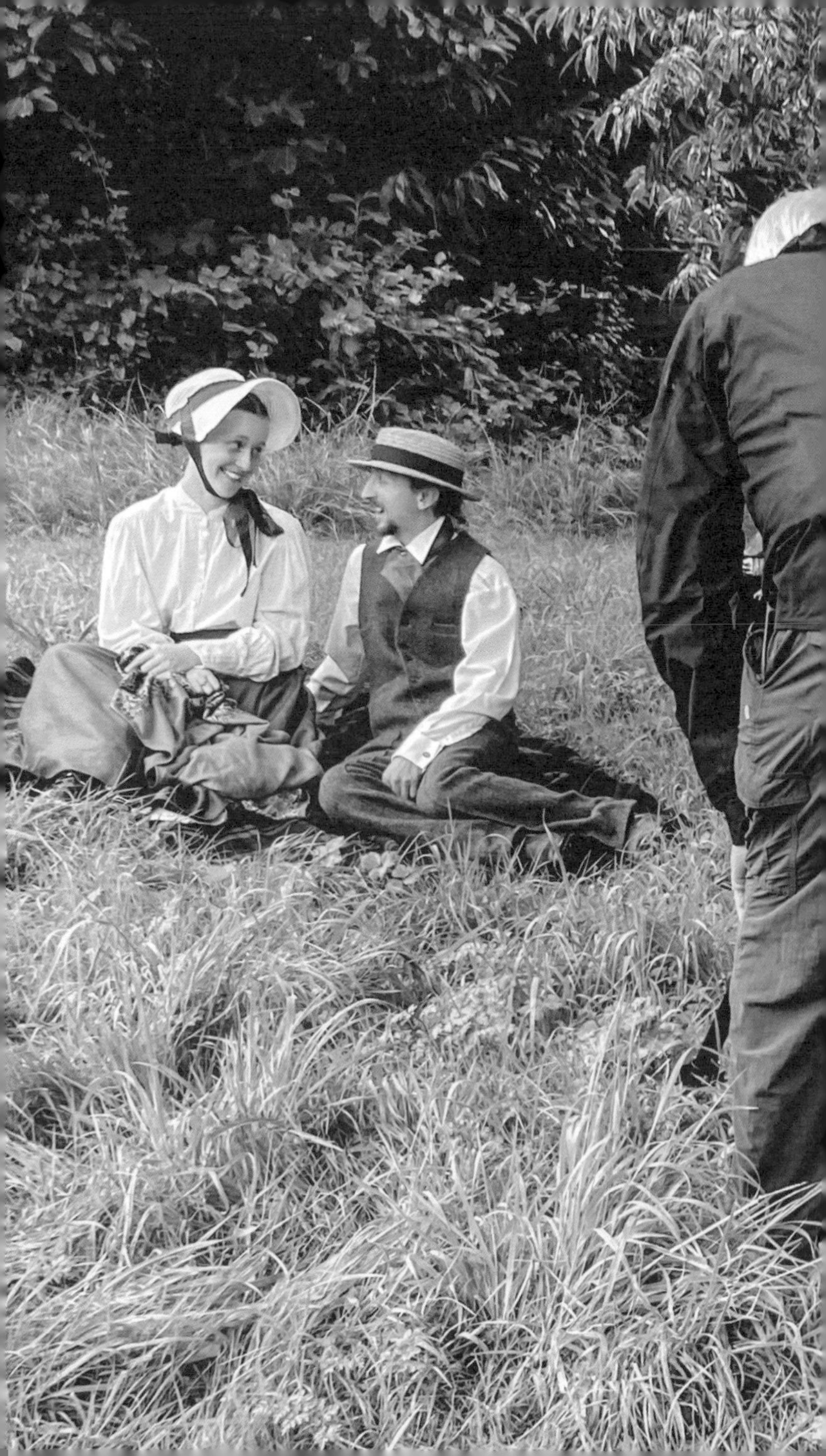

Kate Braidwood and Jonathan White, being directed by Howard Payton with Ian Condon at the camera

Alison Payton as Emma Hardy

Eva Staddon as Eliza Nicholls

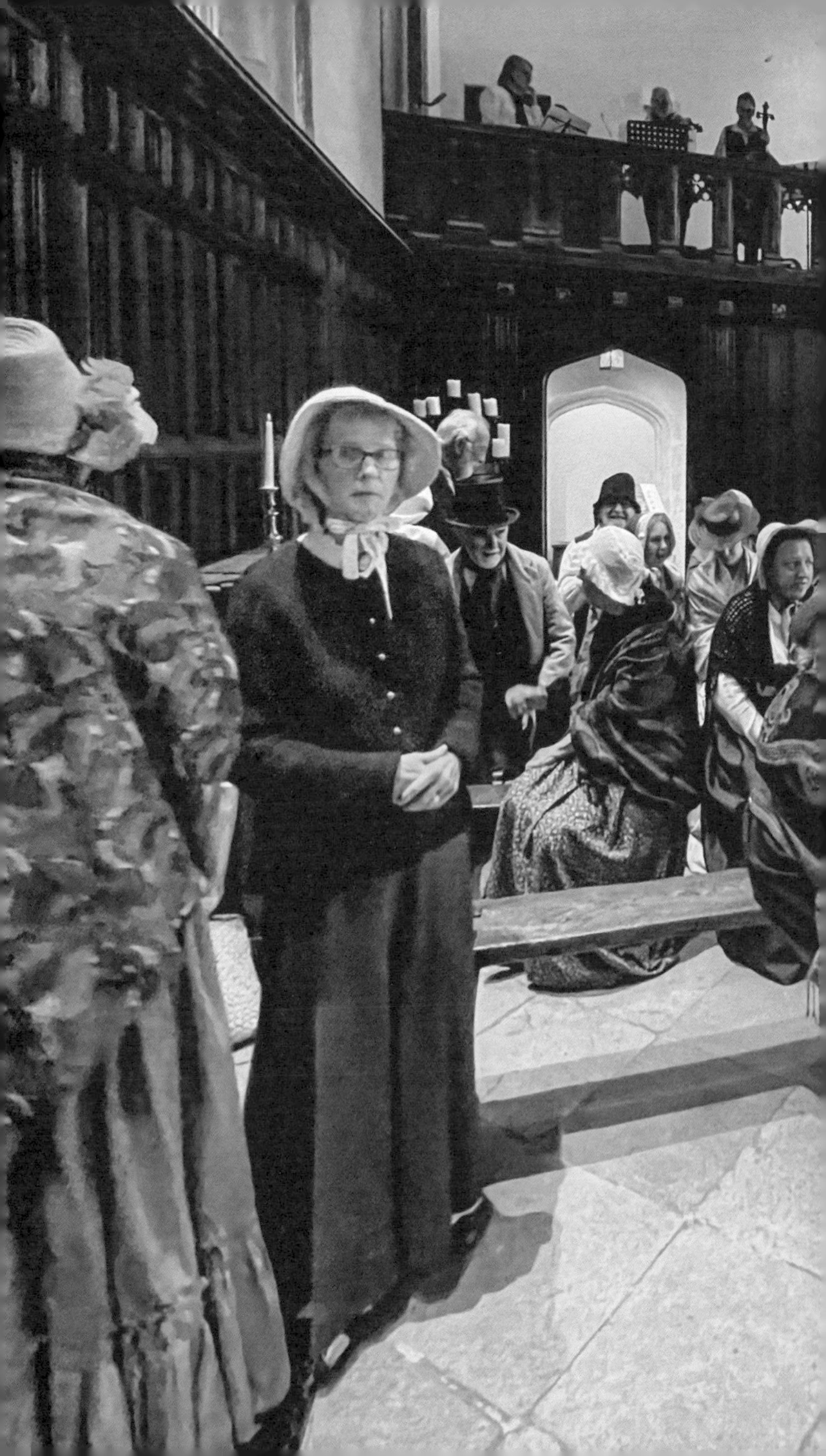

Filming in the Tudor Great Hall at Athelhampton House

Eva Staddon as Mary Jane Nicholls

Bronwyn Fletcher as Retty

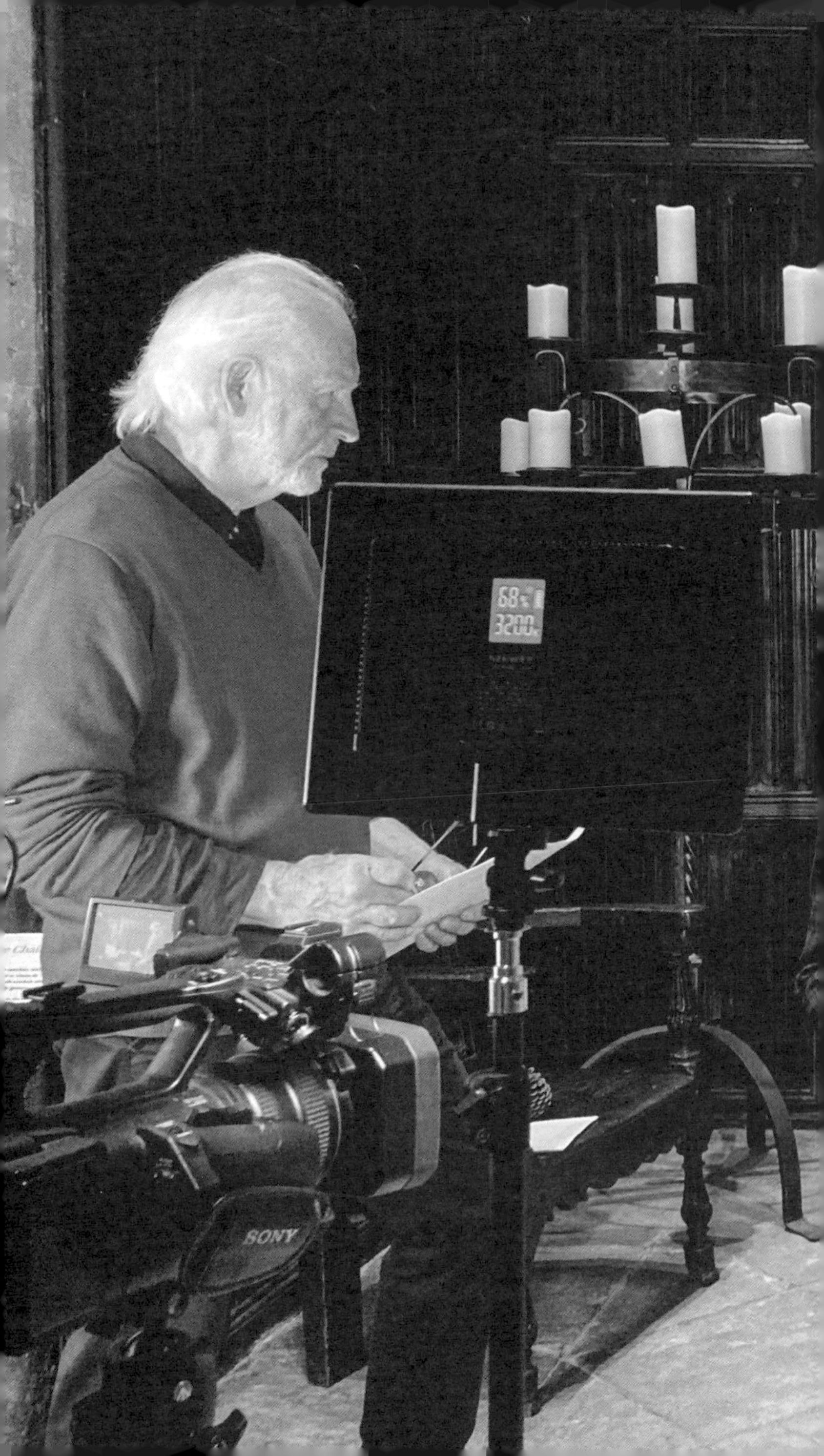
68%
3200K
SONY

Giles Keating interviewing Mark Damon Chutter, directed by Howard Payton

Susie King as Gertrude Bugler

AUTHOR'S NOTE

Most of the material in this book is drawn from the extensive existing body of research on Hardy's poems and romantic life (with full citations in the footnotes). In a few cases, information has been drawn from primarily resources not previously reported by researchers; and existing information has in some areas been reassessed:

1. Elizabeth Bishop (who inspired the poem Lizbie Browne): previous research gives no information on her birth and death dates nor her life after Hardy knew her. The present work has ascertained that she lived from 1837 to 1901, clarifies how much older than Hardy she was, identifies her husband, discusses how she met him, and documents the family they had together.

2. Eliza Nicholls: the only information in existing studies about her life after the end of her engagement to Hardy is that she never married and that she arranged a meeting with him in 1913 after Emma died, apparently hoping to marry him. This book provides more detail about her life and in particular shows that she achieved considerable financial success, bequeathing a substantial sum in her will.

3. Mary Jane Nicholls. Her tragic early death from cancer just a few years after her relationship with Hardy ended, omitted in other studies, is reported.

New information is provided on her husband's career and on his subsequent marriages.

4. Mary Frances Scott-Siddons. This book challenges the assumption in other studies that Hardy had no relationship with her, despite the clear signals in his poems; it also reassess known information about her later career to argue that it was in many respects highly successful.

5. Phena Sparks. Existing research is presented in a way that aims to help readers make up their own minds on the intensity and duration of Hardy's relationship with her and on the controversial issue of whether she became pregnant by him. New analysis of historical meteorological data challenges earlier work suggesting that the unplanned pregnancy described in the poem "The Place on the Map" could not refer to Phena.

ACKNOWLEDGEMENTS

Many thanks to Nicole Sochor and Elizabeth Lowry for their invaluable comments on drafts, to Owen Davies for his outstanding work in layout and preparation, to Noah Warnes for his fabulous line drawings, to Mark Damon Chutter for his excellent Foreword and to Howard Payton for his superb photos of the cast.

Great thanks are also due to all the interviewees, actors, Directors and technical team on the short videos, from whom I've learned so much about Hardy and his poetry, and also to the Hardy Society Committee and members who have been enthusiastic supporters of the project; while all the errors and inadequacies in the book are down to me.

Thank you to those who have helped with the production of the films including, Old Brewery Hall, Ansty, Andy Worth Broadcast and Sound, Keep 106 Local and Community Radio, Owen Davies, Gemma Childs, Emma Park and the team at Athelhampton House & Gardens.

10 LOVERS 50 POEMS

BIBLIOGRAPHY

Argent, A. (1995) 'Thomas Hardy's Schooling', *The Journal of the United Reformed Church History Society*, 5(7), pp. 415-430.

Bailey, J. (1970) The Poetry of Thomas Hardy: A Handbook and Commentary. Chapel Hill: University of North Carolina Press.

Byrne, P. (2024) Hardy Women: Mother, Sisters, Wives, Muses. London: William Collins. ISBN 978-0-00-832225-0

Cox, J. (1963) The Domestic Life of Thomas Hardy 1921-1928 Miss E.E.T. (Hardy's Parlour-Maid). Beaminster, Dorset: Toucan Cox.

Cox, J. (1963a) Thomas Hardy Proposes to Mary Waight. Beaminster, Dorset: Toucan Cox.

Deacon, L. and Coleman, T. (1966) Providence and Mr Hardy. London: Hutchinson & Co.

Fincham, A. (2006) 'Emma Hardy: The (Mad) Woman in the Attic?' The Thomas Hardy Journal, 22, pp. 105-115.

Ford, M. (2023) Woman Much Missed: Thomas Hardy, Emma Hardy and Poetry. Oxford: Oxford University Press. ISBN 978-0-19-288680-4

Gittings, R. (1978) Young Thomas Hardy. Middlesex: Penguin Books.

Hardy, F. (1962) The Life of Thomas Hardy. London: Macmillan.

Hardy, T., ed. Millgate, M. (1984) The Life and Work of Thomas Hardy. London: The Macmillan Press Ltd. ISBN 0-333-29441-6

Hardy, T. (1919) Wessex Poems and Other Verses. London: Macmillan.

Hayes, T. (no date) Jemima Hardy The Great Author's Mother. Available at: https://www.hardysociety.org/articles/jemima-hardy-the-great-authors-mother-by-tracy-hayes/ (Accessed: 18 November 2024)

Hillyard, N. (2014) About Tryphena: Hardy and his young cousin. Peterborough: Fastprint publishing. ISBN 978-178035-778-2

Johnson, B. (2011) Thomas Hardy novelist and poet, his life and work. Available at: https://www.historic-uk.com/CultureUK/Thomas-Hardy/ (Accessed: 18 November 2024)

Johnson, L. (1894) The Art of Thomas Hardy. London: Elkin Matthews and John Lane.

Millgate, M. (1982) Thomas Hardy: A Biography. New York: Random House. ISNB 0-394-48802-4

Millgate, M., ed. (1996) Letters of Emma and Florence Hardy, Oxford: Oxford University Press ISBN 978-0-19-818609-0

Millgate, M. (2004) Thomas Hardy: A Biography Revisited. Oxford: Oxford University Press. ISBN 978-0-19-927566-3

Millgate, M. and Mottram, S. (2010) 'Eliza Bright Nicholls: New source, old problems', The Thomas Hardy Journal 26 pp. 24-34.

Morgan, R (2009) 'Uncollected Items: Florence Dugdale, "Baby Brother"', The Hardy Review, 11(1), pp. 5-11.

Norman, A. (2011) Thomas Hardy: Behind the Mask. Cheltenham: The History Press. ISBN 978-0-75-245630-0

Pascoe, C. (1880) The Dramatic List: A record of the principal performances of living actors and actresses of the British stage. London: Hardwicke and Bogue.

Purdy, R. (1955) The Purdy Hardy Collection. GEN MSS III Box 17, Folder 549. Yale: Beinecke Library.

Purdy, R. ed. Pettit, C. (2002) Thomas Hardy: A Bibliographical Study. Delaware: Oak Knoll Press and London: The British Library. ISBN 1-58456-070-3 (USA) and 0-7123-4766-6 (UK)

Richardson, A. and Angear, H. eds. (2019) Hardy's Correspondents, Phase One. Available at: https://hardycorrespondents.exeter.ac.uk/index.html (Accessed: 18 November 2024)

Richardson, A. ed. (2020) Available at: https://www.dorsetmuseum.org/thomas-hardy-letters-discovered/ (Accessed: 18 November 2024).

Simkin, J. (2020) Available at: https://spartacus-educational.com/JgiffordEH.htm (Accessed: 18 November 2024).

Taylor, D (1999) 'The Chronology of Hardy's Poetry', Victorian Poetry, 37(1), pp. 1-58.

Thomas, J. (2013) 'In defence of Thomas Hardy', The Hardy Society Journal, 9(2), pp. 39–59.

Tomalin, C. (2012) Thomas Hardy The Time-Torn Man, London: Penguin. ISBN 978-0-241-963-28-9

Willard, F. and Livermore, M. (1893). A Woman of the century: 1470 biographical sketches accompanied by portraits of leading American women in all walks of life. New York: Charles Wells Moulton.

Woodhall, N. (2006): Norrie's Tale, an autobiography of the last of the 'Hardy Players'. Wareham: Lullworde Publications. ISBN 978-0-950453-4-5

NOTES

i The "bay-red hair" is quoted in Hardy (1984, p. 30). Hardy's notebook for March 1888 mentions his youthful recollections of "...village beauties…"

ii Elizabeth Bishop's father, Joseph Bishop, is listed as a gamekeeper in the 1851 census and a labourer on the railway in 1861. Marriage and birth certificates show that she married a carpenter, Samuel Charles Harris, in 1860 at Fordington, a suburb of Dorchester, and moved to her husband's county of Berkshire and had three children when she was 38, 41 and 43. Relevant links to the original documents are in the Emma Lloyd family tree, available at (accessed 18 November 2024): https://www.ancestry.co.uk/family-tree/person/tree/79520414/person/38400505521

iii It seems likely that Elizabeth would have met Samuel Charles when he had come to Dorset to work; one possibility is that he was part of the mobile workforce helping with railway construction, with the broad gauge line to Dorchester West opening in 1857 and the standard gauge line eastward from Dorchester South being doubled between 1858 and the early 1860s. If Elizabeth's father had already switched from gamekeeping to railway labouring by then, he might have made the introduction.

iv In addition, "Voices from things growing in a Churchyard" describes her grave. Biographical details for Fanny Hurd are not readily obtainable.

v One example is Louisa Harding, daughter of a local farmer. Hardy describes his feelings for her in "To Louisa in the Lane", written in 1927 just before his death: see Taylor (1999, p. 56, entry for 1927), while "The Passer-By" is written as though from Louisa's standpoint: see Millgate (1982, p. 58). Hardy (1962, p. 26), says that "Good evening" were the only words that passed between them, but Hardy (1984, p. 30) also claims that they additionally "used to meet" when he was in his early 20s.

vi "Famously" and the earlier quote in this paragraph about Jemima's independence are taken from Hayes (no date).

vii Most of the biographical details for Eliza, Mary Jane and their relatives are taken from the English birth, census, death and probate records. A summary giving links to the relevant documents is available on the Preece/Price Walton/Cowley family tree, within which the links to Eliza's documents are given at https://www.ancestry.co.uk/family-tree/person/tree/6217559/person/6013423768 A document link missing from this source is for Eliza in the 1861 census, which shows her temporarily staying at her employer's in-laws at Godstone on the day of the census: see: https://www.ancestry.co.uk/discoveryui-content/view/6867751:8767 (both links acccesed 18 November 2024). When interpreting Eliza's age as shown on census records, note she was born on 28th November 1840 in Fishergate in Brighton and then baptised in the parish church of Findon, her mother's family's village, on 27th December 1840.

viii   Eliza's employer, whose family was also based in Purbeck, gave her a book which she subsequently gave to Hardy. It was a copy of The Christian Year which he used as a diary, first entry in April 1861, a year before he left Dorset for London. See Millgate and Mottram (2010, pp. 24-34). See Byrne (2024, pp. 141-2) for analysis of Eliza and Hardy's likely meeting while he restored a church in Coombe Keynes in the Isle of Purbeck area of Dorset.

ix   Mary Waight was seven years older than Hardy and worked in The Mantle Showroom, Dorchester, the "Best Business in Town". She went on to marry George Oliver. One of her grandchildren, Constance Oliver, describes Hardy's proposal in a long interview; for these biographical details see Cox (1963a). The rejected proposal of marriage occurred in early 1862 and Hardy moved to London that April, so the gap between the two events cannot have been long and may have been very short.

x   This description of Eliza Nicholls's relationship with Hardy is based on the testimony of her niece, Sarah Headley, who in 1955 reported it to Professor Richard Purdy. See Purdy (1955) and the summary Jane in Byrne (2024, pp. 140-1 and 156-7). Headley also refers to Hardy switching his affections to Eliza's sister, Mary Jane: see Bryne (p158 and note 7 p 610).

xi   Hardy emphasises that Eliza is the subject of these poems by illustrating "She to Him I" in the 1898 Wessex Poems edition with a sketch showing two figures on a winding road leading towards a silhouette that appears to be Clavell Tower. This stands on a headland near the sea in Dorset a few hundred metres from the coastguard cottages where Eliza was living with her family when he first met her.

xii   Millgate (1982, p. 94) suggests this poem relates to Eliza, and others have followed this interpretation.

xiii   Johnson (1894, p. 135) notes that the anapaestic (three-syllable end-stressed) metre, though sometimes seen in folk songs, was more common in comic music-hall forms.

xiv   See Millgate (1982, p. 494), and Byrne (2024, p. 508), who describes Eliza as "broken-hearted" after the 1913 meeting with Hardy.

xv   See the sources in note vii. The calculated lower figure is based on applying the rise in the UK retail prices index from 1918 to 2023, the higher figure uses the Bank of England's long run house price index. Eliza did not obtain these funds as a bequest from her father, whose probate record shows all his effects left to a local Findon farmer, Albert Short (1845-1931); it is possible that she benefitted from transfers from him during his lifetime, but if so, those could be seen as a form of payment for her work in his pub.

xvi   There seems little or no primary evidence about the timing of the relationship between Hardy and Mary Jane. As regards its start, Millgate (1982, pp. 94 and 100-101) suggests that it developed gradually as Hardy and Eliza were breaking up. For its end, he argues

NOTES

that Mary Jane "soon bestowed her affections elsewhere" but the only documented information is that she married Harry Beach in 1869, and it seems likely that she would have courted him for some time beforehand. It also seems probable that her relationship with Hardy would have ended by April 1867 when he was briefly involved with Mrs Scott-Siddons.

xvii In Hardy's poetry collection Time's Laughingstocks, first published in 1904, a note underneath "Her Definition" dates it to Summer 1866 and locates it at W.P.V., his London lodgings at 16 Westbourne Park Villas. This date was likely when his relationship with Mary Jane was going well, so it is reasonable to believe this happy poem, praising the object of his love, is about her. It is most unlikely that Hardy is referring to Eliza, given that around this time he was also composing the "She, to Him" sequence describing their bitter break-up.

xviii See the sources listed in the first note to this chapter. Harry remarried twice more, having children with his fourth wife.

xix W. P. V. refers to Westbourne Park Villas, where Hardy has his lodgings at this time. He sometimes wrote this out fully at the end of his poems, sometimes gave only the initials, and sometimes included the street number, which was 16.

xx Purdy (2002, p. 143) identifies Scott-Siddons as the actress referenced in both this and the following poem, confirming the date of the performance. The only other possibility, Mrs Hermann Vezin, is effectively ruled out since there is no record of her playing Rosalind that year until September 4th (https://www.umass.edu/AdelphiTheatreCalendar/m66d.htm#Label014) (assessed 18 November 2024).

xxi For summaries of Scott-Siddons's career, see Pascoe (1880, pp. 277-278), which includes extensive quotes from newspaper reviews of the performance of Rosalind that Hardy described, and Willard and Livermore (1893, p. 656).

xxii Purdy (2002, p.143) and Byrne (2024, p. 167) wonder if Hardy's "The Two Rosalinds", published in 1909, might refer to Mrs Scott-Siddons. But the dates in this poem do not fit the reality of her life: the performance cited for 1863 would have taken place before her career had started while that "some forty years" later would have been around 1903, many years after her death in 1896. If Hardy did intend this poem to refer to her, it seems he deliberately chose implausible dates, perhaps to signal an impressionistic lament for the passing of a former lover rather than a description of reality.

xxiii Athelhampton school had been founded by George and Mary Wood, who had owned the estate since 1848. Mary was from the Vaizey family, leading Nonconformists in the early to mid-Victorian era. The school was directly across the road from Athelhampton House: see Argent (1995, p. 421). Deacon and Coleman (1966, p. 33) cite as evidence of Phena's attendance at Athelhampton School a story book, still existing: *Matty Gregg, or The Woman that did What She Could.* published by the Religious Tract Society and with an inscription on the fly leaf: "Presented to Tryphena Sparks for attention to her duties as Monitor at the Athelhampton School, August 14th 1862".

xxiv Deacon and Coleman (1966), who carried out the extended interview with Phena's daughter Nellie (formal names Eleanor Tryphena), describe the relationship between Hardy and Phena as a "love affair" (p. 25) and say they "became lovers" (p. 31). They also say (p. 26) "Of Hardy's courtship of Tryphena in Dorset in 1867 and 1868 Nellie knew little except that they took long walks together, and became engaged." Consistent with this, Bailey (1970, p. 40) comments that in 1940, Miss Irene Cooper Willis, friend of Florence Dugdale and lawyer for the Trustees of the Hardy estate, noted that Hardy had an "understanding" with a "girl of his own countryside" prior to proposing to Emma, on whom he had bestowed the ring intended for the discarded maiden. Byrne (2024, p.220) suggests that the ring given to Emma may have been intended for Cassie Pole.

xxv If the pregnancy referenced in the poem was Phena's and did go to full term, it would relate to the child that Deacon and Coleman (1966, pp. 182-196) suggest that Phena and Hardy had together; see the photo (accessed 21 November 2024) at http://www.montford-productions.co.uk/My%20Lost%20Prize/Randy.htm. Among alternative views, Byrne (2024, p. 223) believes the poem refers to Hardy's sojourn with Emma in summer 1870. However, this lasted only three weeks in August so is difficult to reconcile with the poem looking back from the "latter summer" to a period of "weeks and weeks" prior. Pinion (1976, p. 98) argues that Cornwall fits the landscape description in the poem better than Dorset, but adds that it is "difficult to interpret" it as referring to Emma. He instead cites research by Robert Gittings (reference unclear) showing that "the only fine hot Indian summer from 1865 to 1875 was in the year 1865", suggesting it refers to a child of Henry Moule's that may have been fathered in that year. The source for Gittings's data is not clear and information for Southampton, the nearest meteorological station to Dorset, seems consistent with the poem referring to Hardy and Phena's time together in summer 1867. It shows the maximum temperature that September as 19 degrees, fractionally warmer than the average for the previous twelve years (which is as far back as data are available). The poem also refers to a lack of rain for "weeks and weeks" before the "latter summer", so perhaps referring to August, for which month in 1867 the data show rainfall of 53mm, some 8mm (about one standard error) less than the twelve-year average. Data accessed 20 November 2024: https://www.metoffice.gov.uk/pub/data/weather/uk/climate/stationdata/southamptondata.txt.

xxvi The headmistress called a school assembly, focussed on the seventh commandment (Thou shalt not commit adultery), just a few days after Phena left. See Hillyard (2014, p. 134). This was not the normal subject-matter for school assembly and its choice suggests that Phena was sacked because of her relationship with Hardy; possibly also because the headmistress had become aware that she was (or had been) pregnant. The delay of about 8 months before she took up her new job at a nonconformist school may have been simply because she had to wait for the start of the new academic year. Or, had she been pregnant, it would have offered a convenient break for her to go somewhere else to have the baby discreetly and give him to others to be brought up, an outcome not unusual among unmarried mothers at the time. (Hillyard, p. 135, wonders whether a reference in Hardy's posthumously published and self-authored biography to a vanished lyric about "A Departure by Train" that February might relate to this.) It seems unlikely that this could have happened without the knowledge and support of Mary Wood and others in the Nonconformist group based at Athelhampton, since they found Phena the new job at the right time; they already knew how promising she was as a teacher, and may have been keen to ensure that her career prospects were not ruined.

xxvii Gittings (1978, p174)

xxviii Hardy signalled who "Her Initials" refers to by providing an accompanying drawing containing letters that can be read as either T.S. or P.S. – Tryphena or Phena Sparks.

xxix This quote is from Gittings (1978, p. 177). Other poems from this era that might refer to the break-up between Hardy and Phena include "At Waking", "The Wind's Prophecy" and perhaps "Singing Lovers". Millgate (1982, p. 120) wonders if the first two of these as well as "Her Initials" might relate to the break-up with Eliza Nicholls, though this seems unlikely given the initials mentioned in the previous note, and also their total contrast in tone compared with the "She, to Him" series. Gittings (1978, pp. 176-77) also mentions "In the Vaulted Way" as possibly relating to the break-up with Phena.

xxx Consistent with the break-up being an "ambiguous parting", Hardy (1984, p. 66), refers to there being "flirtation" at the dancing-classes in Weymouth. While there are questions over the credibility of this part of his (auto)biography given that it makes no mention of Phena at all (apart from a brief indirect reference in respect of a much later period in Hardy's life), Millgate (1982, p. 119) argues that the poems "Her Father" and "The Dawn After the Dance" may refer to flirtations at this time.

xxxi Deacon and Coleman (1966, p. 39) suggest that Hardy and Phena had meetings as late as 1871, when he had already started courting Emma; were this is correct, the rules of the teacher-training college would have restricted them to occasional afternoon walks in the streets of south London.

xxxii Cassie (Catherine) Pole was a lady's maid at Kingston Maurward House. Her involvement with Hardy is mentioned by biographers including Millgate (1982, p.149), and Byrne (2024), who suggests that he was watched by her from her window on the day he left for his three-day trip to Cornwall (p. 214), was snubbed later by her father for having slighted his daughter (p. 196), and wrote a poem that may relate to her death in London (p. 197). Some reports say that he gave Cassie a ring, possibly the same one previously given to Phena and later given to Emma.

xxxiii Deacon and Coleman (1966, p. 40).

xxxiv In one edition, Hardy abbreviated "Phena" to "Ph...a" and in another he renamed the poem as "Thoughts at News of a Woman's Death". He also destroyed some journal entries relating to this period (see Bailey, 1970). One interpretation is that his relationship with Phena had been so strong that it was a sensitive subject that he preferred not to draw attention to.

xxxv Deacon and Coleman (1966, p. 64).

xxxvi Hardy (1984, p.77).

xxxvii This analysis is drawn from Byrne (2024, pp. 223-4), who also argues that the pregnancy referred to in "The Place on the Map" relates not to Phena but to Emma (who has no recorded baby, so by implication it would have been a false alarm, or a miscarriage). However, it's not clear that the three weeks Hardy and Emma spent together in August 1870 was long enough to match the time description in that poem (see footnote xxv).

xxxviii Hardy (1984 p. 86).

xxxix Hardy (1984, p. 119), entry for August 13th 1877: "We hear that Jane, our late servant, is soon to have a baby. Yet never a sign of one is there for us." A month earlier, the entry for July 13th probably refers to the same topic: "The sudden disappointment of a hope leaves a scar…"

xl This is a quote from notes made on the manuscript version of volume II of Hardy's Life, as reported by Taylor (1999, p. 41, note to year 1893).

xli The subtitle, "A Reminiscence, 1893" is unusual for Hardy in making clear that this is based on a remembrance of an actual event, and the date provides a strong signal of who his companion was. He delayed publication of this poem until 1914, after the death of Emma. Purdy (1955, p. 345) states that Mrs (Florence) Hardy associated this poem and "A Broken Appointment" with Florence Henniker.

xlii Long afterwards Florence Hardy (neé Dugdale) wrote in a letter to a friend: "Wessex Heights will always wring my heart, for I know when it was written a little while after the publication of *Jude*, when he was so cruelly treated."

xliii This poem is associated with Florence Henniker by Mrs (Florence) Hardy, see note above.

xliv Richardson and Angear (2019, "Thomas Hardy to Florence Henniker, 11th August 1911").

xlv Tomalin (2012, p. 343). However, note that Ford (2023, p. 132), believes this poem refers to Emma.

xlvi Byrne (2024, p. 443).

xlvii Letter from Thomas Hardy to Florence Henniker, 1896.

xlviii Source: for the quote: Simkin (2020). Christine was daughter of the house at Athelhampton until 1891 when her father sold it to Alfred Cart de Lafontaine, see 1891 census referenced at (accessed 18 November 2024) : https://www.ancestry.co.uk/family-tree/person/tree/118868767/person/172155527650

xlix See, for example, Fincham (2006).

l Purdy (2002, p.200) says that Hardy added this in his final revision to Moments of Vision, 1917, in which this poem was published.

li These poems were published in 1917, after Emma's death; it is not clear when they were written. So, the comment on love and respect could apply to her directly, or to her memory

NOTES

lii   Letter from Emma to Betty Owen, April 1899.

liii   The Sphere had just been founded by Clement Shorter as a direct rival to The Illustrated London News, of which he had previously been editor, and Emma's poem appeared in his "A Literary Letter" column. The Academy and Literature was published between 1869 and 1915 (sometimes appearing under a slightly different title).

liv   Johnson (1894, p. 226), describes this as "one of the most moving transitions anywhere in English poetry."

lv   See Tomalin (2012, pp. 312-3), who claims that Lilian invited herself and was not welcomed by Hardy, Kate or Florence.

lvi   Source: Morgan (2009, p. 5).

lvii   *The Dynasts*, Hardy's epic poem about the Napoleonic Wars, in locations from Moscow to Vienna and back to the hills around his home, runs to 600 pages in the three-volume 1927 edition, published by Macmillan & Co, London.

lviii   "After the Visit" was first published in The Spectator in 1910, then in Satires of Circumstance in 1914 with the dedication to F.E.D. added. See Tomalin (2012, p. 435, note 6).

lix   Some years later, after Emma had died and Hardy had remarried, Florence Henniker referred to this alliteration when she wrote to Hardy: "I have read a great many poems and... very especially do I like the one to Florence. There are such lovely lines in that…the 'large luminous living eyes'." See Richardson and Angear (2019, letter Florence Henniker to Thomas Hardy, 25th November 1914).

lx   As described in Hardy's collected letters, conveniently referenced in Ford (2023, p. 205).

lxi   "At the Departure Gate" was published in 1909 in *Time's Laughingstocks*, so though written later than "After the Visit", it was published slightly earlier. Source for Dugdale connection to this poem: Purdy (2002, p.161).

lxii   Evidence for these various meetings come from Hardy's collected letters and are summarised in Ford (2023, p. 205).

lxii   In 1910 they published jointly "Blue Jimmy: The Horse-Stealer", and Hardy supported Florence's work on *The Book of Baby Birds*, published a couple of years later.

lxiv   The Lyceum Club was founded by writer and journalist Constance Smedley in 1903 to provide women with an interest in the arts an alternative to the male-only clubs widespread at that time, and a network of sister clubs subsequently opened up across 17 countries. See https://lyceumclublondon.org

lxv   For the meeting and subsequent interaction of Florence Dugdale and Emma, see Ford (2023, pp. 205, 210-4). The return visits to the Clodd home are reported on p. 208.

lxvi   Hardy (1984, p. 394).

lxvii   As an example, Hardy's journal records visits with Florence to Athelhampton in 1921, 1922 and 1923. Their hosts, Mr and Mrs Cochrane, had purchased the house in 1919 and built a fine new rear wing. See Taylor (1999, pp. 52, 60 and 74).

lxviii   Cox (1963, Q&A section).

lxix   See Millgate (2004, p. 513).

lxx   Cox (1963, p. 14). Additionally, the maid described the overall mood at Max Gate as "...depressing. No joy in the house, nobody really happy." However, May O'Rourke, Hardy's secretary, wrote in 1926, "This is my third year with you, and dear Mrs Hardy, and Wessie [the dog], and I can frame no better wish than that the years ahead will make you as happy as my three years at Max Gate have made me. See Richardson and Angear (2019, letter May O'Rourke to Thomas Hardy, 1st June 1926).

lxxi   Cox (1963, p. 16).

lxxxii   Richardson (2020, quoting a letter from Florence Hardy to Harold Barlow, 1932).

lxxiv   Letter from Florence to Sydney Cockrell, 26th Dec 1920, Millgate (1996, p. 171).

lxxiv   Richardson and Angear (2019, letter from Gertrude Bugler to ThomasHardy, 4th February 1925).

lxxv   For the interview, see (accessed 7 March 2025) https://www.youtube.com/watch?v=q0oe7J4FKp8. The description in this chapter is largely based on the oral history from that interview, and from Gertrude's sister Norrie, in Woodhall (2006, pp.23-34). See also Byrne (2024, pp. 527-550).

lxxvi   Information about the films that Hardy was involved with in his lifetime are available at https://thebioscope.net/2008/04/29/pen-and-pictures-no-1-thomas-hardy/ and references therein (accessed 11th April 2025).

OTHER PUBLICATIONS

Anne of Athelhampton and the Riddle of the Apes
Giles Keating

Anne of Athelhampton and the Queen's Pearls
Giles Keating

Anne of Athelhampton Colouring Book
illustrated by Noah Warnes

The Visitation to Athelhampton
*Alfred Cart de Lafontaine,
preface and notes Owen Davies*

Athelhampton, The House
Owen Davies

Athelhampton, The Gardens
Sophy Robertson & Owen Davies

Athelhampton House nestles in the heart of Dorset, a few miles east of the county town of Dorchester. It is considered one of the finest examples of Tudor domestic architecture in England. When you visit the house and gardens, you can see many of the locations where the videos were filmed, such as the small meadow by the Tollhouse where Hardy strolled with Retty, the walk along the River Piddle where "Two Year Idyll" and other Sturminster poems were filmed, or the Grey Parlour where the sinister figure "At the Piano" was shot.

The house and its gardens welcome visitors across all seasons of the year. For current opening times, please visit www.athelhampton.com or telephone 01305 848363